Rave Reviews for To

An intelligent, thoughtful treatment of a too-frequently neglected issue. This book should be helpful to students and parents alike.

STEPHEN SINGER,
College Counselor, The Horace Mann School

Taking time off was the best decision I ever made!

TRACY JOHNSTON
Wellesley College, Class of '95

One of the best books written to help students become familiar with how successfully to take time off from school.

TED SPENCER
Director, Office of Undergraduate Admissions
University of Michigan

A year off either before or during college is not for everyone. However, Taking Time Off *offers some convincing options for this worthwhile experience. An interesting read.*

CAROL KATZ
College Advisor, Stuyvesant High School

We all start life as butterflies and usually end up in cocoons. On the other hand, we could take the advice of Colin Hall and Ron Lieber and have our mid-life crisis while we are young enough to enjoy it! I can think of no better testimonial to the value of sabbaticals from college than the accounts collected in Taking Time Off.

CORNELIUS BULL
President & Founder
Center for Interim Programs

Austin,

I support anything you choose to do. You have a very strong sense of purpose.

Love,
Dad

Taking
Time Off

"When a man does not know
what harbor he is making for,
no wind is the right wind."—

— Lucius Annaeus Seneca

Taking
Time Off

Colin Hall and Ron Lieber

Random House, Inc.
New York
www.PrincetonReview.com

Princeton Review Publishing, L. L. C.

2315 Broadway

New York, NY 10024

E-mail: bookeditor@review.com

ISBN 0-375-76303-1

Editorial Director: Robert Franek

Editor: Erik Olson

Designer: Scott Harris

Production Editor: Julieanna Lambert

Production Coordinator: Greta Englert

9 8 7 6 5 4 3 2 1

2nd Edition

Acknowledgments

Many people took time off from their busy lives to help us complete this book. To begin with, we would like to give a special thanks to Joel Zemans. When we came to him in the fall of 1993, our enthusiasm for this book was our only collateral. Joel gave us a loan anyway, and his generosity enabled us to travel around the country to conduct our interviews.

Early on, Elisa Tamarkin and Kim Townsend convinced us that a book proposal was not the same thing as a five-paragraph essay. Ben Lieber and Susan Little dispensed excellent advice on what a book like this should include. Mary Berger and Norman Newell gave us valuable advice on self-publishing. We must also thank Michael Lee Cohen, Ted Conover, and Chris Ogden, who convinced us that we needed an agent and helped us find one.

We owe appreciation to Mike DeBeer, whose computer expertise enabled us to flood the Internet with our request for stories from people who had taken time off. When we hit the road to start tracking people down in person, a number of people put us up or put up with us. Thanks to David Korduner and Joan Krimston, Josh and Celine Krimston, Fran and Monte Krimston, the Quezadas and the Steeles, and Christina Hall and Peter Wald. We are also grateful to the people at Jenner & Block, especially Sharon Webb and Joan Gill, who helped us in innumerable ways while we were completing the manuscript. Carrie Bader, Mandy Field, Erin Kaufman, Jennifer Mattson, Sarah Nasonchuk, and Ilya Somin all noticed mistakes in the manuscript that had eluded us. When our General Resources section needed a third set of eyes, Barbara Messing stepped in and brought it to a whole new level.

Colin: I would especially like to thank my mother, Joan Hall, who provides me with constant support and encouragement in everything that I do. Her parents, Warren and Delia McClurg, always kept a map of the world tacked to the wall in their home. They would stick colored pins in one country after another every time they received a postcard or phone call from one of their children or grandchildren who were working or traveling or studying abroad. I can't send my grandparents postcards anymore, but I hope they know what a great impact they have had on everyone in our family.

George Cotsirilos and his family have brought my mother and the rest of our family many years of love and happiness and Greek food for which we are all very grateful. I am glad Christina Hall and Peter Wald will have a chance to share a new and improved version of this book with Gideon, Elias, and Cassidy. Along with Lynn Hall, they have made San Francisco feel like home. Jim and Lori McClurg make Nebraska feel like home and always give me the best advice. My brother Justin is the real writer in the family, and I am so proud of the person he has become. I also feel lucky to have such good friends from my time at Francis W. Parker, Amherst, Morgan Stanley, Rhône, and Stanford.

Ron: A special tip of the cap to Terry Allen, who opened the pages of *Amherst* magazine to me. I'm also grateful to Ann Jones, who encouraged me to take my work to an even wider audience, and to Stan Moulton and Debra Scherban, who gave me some terrific opportunities at the *Daily Hampshire Gazette*. I wouldn't be where I am today without the help of some of the world-class editors I've met since, at *Lawyers Weekly USA*, *Fortune*, *Fast Company*, and *The Wall Street Journal*. Thanks especially to Edward Felsenthal and Eben Shapiro at *The Journal*, who saw through my haphazard thicket of journalistic interests (like this one) and gave me a shot on the *Personal Journal* team.

Neither of us would be where we are today without our teachers at the Francis W. Parker School in Chicago. During our fourteen years there, they promoted a vision of an education that extended beyond the four walls of the classroom. We hope the spirit behind Parker's progressive education is reflected in the stories we have collected for this book. In particular, we owe appreciation to Harriett Cholden, John Cotton, Barnaby Dinges, Joel Dure, Bill Duffy, Diane Fitzgerald, Dan Frank, Dren Geer, Karen Harrison, Andy Kaplan, Connie Kelly, Bernard Markwell, Pat McHale, Bob Merrick, Bonnie Seebold, Marie Stone, and Roger Wallenstein.

We have many friends in common whose support and encouragement we would like to recognize. Kate Alberg, Josh Anderson, Christine Bader, Matt Brown, the Buchanan family, Steve Burwell, Megan Carr, Derek Coppoletti, Katerina Christopoulos, Al Decker, Phil Dur, Jim Feldman, Rachel Gordon, Tom Goundrey, Doug Guthrie, Kim Kamin, Eric Klinenberg, Seoni Llanes, Melanie Nutter, Mike Ogden, Agnieszka Pfeiffer, Audrey Prins-Patt, Jeff Posternak, Marc Saiontz, Meghan Searl, Matt Siegel, Owen Steams, Andrew Sweet, Graham Weaver, Deborah Wexler, Eric Wilmes, Charlie Yoon, and Nick Zerbib have all given us immeasurable support throughout this project.

When we first called Anne Edelstein, she had recently become a mother for the first time. We asked her to adopt us, she agreed, and having her as our agent was invaluable. This never would have happened without her. Thanks also to the gang at Farrar, Straus & Giroux for giving a couple of unknown kids their first crack at the book world. We were thrilled to meet John Katzman in 1996, for we had a hunch that his brand of iconoclasm would mesh well with our punk approach to the college matriculation process. He kept his word to publish our book anytime anywhere, and seven years later here we are. Thanks for giving us a new home, John.

The pirates on John's ship at The Princeton Review, Rob Franek and Erik Olson, have been smart, savvy, and thankfully forgiving with deadlines. Plus, they were kind enough to match us up with the amazing Nathan Firer, who did great things with a hopelessly out-of-date General Resources section. We'll save him from law school yet. Thanks to the shrewd, sincere, and enthusiastic Random House duo of Tom Russell and Jeanne Krier for spearheading our publicity efforts. We're thrilled to be in such able hands. Also, thanks be to Christy Fletcher, Ron's new agent, who was a rock throughout a truly unbelievable 2001.

The best part of writing this book was meeting the people we profiled. They invited two perfect strangers into their lives and trusted us to do justice to their stories. There would, quite literally, be no book without them.

We've shared most everything since we shared a kindergarten teacher back in 1974, so it's only fitting that we both feel blessed to have Jodi Kantor in our lives. When Ron has lost all patience for Colin, it's Jodi who brings us both back down to earth. Sometimes, Colin calls just to talk to her and doesn't even ask for Ron anymore. That's okay with Ron, though, since he gets to actually marry her. Jodi, we love you. But Ron loves you the most.

Finally, we would like to thank our families (you too, Kantors!), who have always loved, supported, and most of all, believed in us. We're thrilled that Colin's brother took our advice and jumped off the treadmill at Swarthmore and that Gideon may soon do the same. As for Stephanie and David, all is forgiven. Besides, it's never too late to take time off.

To our families

CONTENTS

PART 1: Work

PART 2: Volunteer

PART 3: Study

PART 4: Travel

"A journey of a thousand miles begins with one step."

—Lao Tsu

Preface

If you could be doing anything you wanted right now, what would it be?

Would you be hiking the Appalachian Trail from Maine to Georgia? Would you be teaching in Africa? Would you be an aide on a presidential campaign? Would you be working for a year or two in the real world, earning money and gaining valuable experience? Or would you be in school?

There is no rule requiring everyone to go straight to college after twelve years of school and then graduate in four years. Each year, tens of thousands of students leave school temporarily to work, travel, volunteer, or just do something different. We hope that by the time you finish reading this book you will see how many incredible things there are to do in the world. Being in college is only one of them.

We discovered the value of taking time off through personal experience. After fourteen years together at the Francis W. Parker School in Chicago, Ron went straight to Amherst College and graduated in four years. Now, he wishes he had spent a year volunteering or traveling before he started his freshman year. Colin, on the other hand, spent a year working and used the money he earned to take a yearlong trip around the world before going to college. It was the best decision he ever made.

When Colin joined Ron at Amherst two years later, a friend came to him for advice. After struggling mightily as a pre-med student, Matt wanted to take a year off to reconsider his academic options. Wisely, he figured that it would be better to get away for a while than to wander aimlessly through the Amherst curriculum at $25,000 a year in search of something that grabbed him. But where, he wondered, could he find the information he needed to plan his time off? Books were available that offered a Yellow Pages–style catalog of things to do, but he thought they were more confusing and intimidating than helpful. What he really wanted was a book of people—living, breathing examples—to prove to him and to his doubting parents that real students had taken time off and thrived as a result. And, most importantly, he wanted to find out *how* they did it.

We decided to write that book, and we spent the next five years putting it together. In order to make the book useful to as many students as possible, we collected the stories of a diverse group of people from all over the country. To cast a wide net, we sent out an e-mail chain letter, which was forwarded around the world. We also placed classified ads in college newspapers around the country, asking people to contact us if they knew anyone who had taken time off. We heard from more than 500 people, and dozens more wrote or called and said they wished our book had been around when they were applying to college. Many people had taken time off before going to college, but others did so during their undergraduate years. We wrote this book with both possibilities in mind, drawing on the range of experiences that people shared with us.

We hope that you will read all of these profiles, including those of people who did things that you would never think of doing yourself. Certain themes are common here: parents, money, when to leave, and why. These issues can be complicated, and our interviewees dealt with them in many different ways. You may find useful information in an unexpected place.

We have arranged the profiles by subject into four sections: Work, Volunteer/Community Service, Study, and Travel/Outdoor Adventure.

At the end of the book, you'll find an index of publications and the names, websites, and telephone numbers of programs and organizations that you might find helpful, including those mentioned by the people we interviewed. You can write to us via Ron's e-mail at ronlieber@yahoo.com, or check out our website at www.takingtimeoff.com. Please let us know what happened when you took time off, how you used our advice, and what we might mention in the next edition of the book.

The people we profiled accomplished an incredible variety of things. They didn't have any strings to pull or much money to throw around. Instead, through sheer force of will and a hefty dose of creativity and verve, they were able to create amazing opportunities for themselves—many of them completely out of thin air. You can, too.

As for our friend Matt, the one who inspired us to write this book, he's a great example of how life can sometimes come more than full circle after a year off. He worked for several months as a forest ranger in New Mexico and then rode his bike through New Zealand. He came back to Amherst, majored in American studies, and then went to work for the Wilderness Society, a conservation organization, as an Alaska-based staff member. But he never kicked his jones for medicine. He volunteered in a hospital up there, then returned to the classroom to complete his pre-med courses. After nearly flunking his college science classes the first time around, Matt will graduate from Stanford Medical School this spring.

So Why Take Time Off?

If you even bothered to pick this book up, you probably already have a hunch that going straight from high school to college and graduating in four years is not the path you want to take. Generally, this feeling crops up for a couple of reasons. Some people don't get into the colleges they want to attend, so they take a year off and reapply the following year. More and more often, top schools are admitting students but asking them to take a semester or year off before they start because there isn't room for them on campus. Other students realize they've made a bad choice of schools or majors and want to take a year to regroup, like our friend Matt. Then there's the group that sees some incredible opportunity in front of them that they may never have again and grabs it. They volunteer on a political campaign, work for a start-up, train for the Olympics, or pursue some other particular skill or talent. Or, most often, people simply run out of money and need to take time off and work to make more of it.

Sometimes, people work so hard trying to take every AP course, participate in every extracurricular activity, and buzz through the summer working or studying further, that they're simply burnt out when high school ends. This doesn't elicit much sympathy from the adults in their life, who generally can't take a sabbatical themselves. But you can, and you should if you're so inclined. The assembly line that carries you straight from high school to college and out into the real world moves quickly, so jumping off takes courage. And we're not here to judge you on which reasons are right and which ones are wrong.

The simple fact is, if you're not ready to be in college, then you shouldn't go. Attending college when you are not ready or not excited to be there can be a tremendous waste. The typical advice you'll hear is, "Just go! College is great, and if you don't like it, you can do something else after your first year. But at least give it a chance." The legitimate fear here is that life is complicated and that everyone will be faced with many difficult choices. Parents hope that by shipping you directly off to college and keeping you there, they will help make some of those choices for you. That, you may remember, was the idea behind arranged marriages. But today, at upwards of $35,000 a year for tuition, room, and board, is "give it a chance" a chance that is really worth taking?

Your family may have genuine and strongly held convictions about the value of graduating from college as soon as possible, getting a job, and establishing yourself as an independent, financially self-sufficient person. These convictions are entirely reasonable, and they may lead your family to feel that taking time off is irresponsible. Your challenge is to articulate exactly what it is that you want to do and why. If you can show your family why you'd be able to take advantage of college more fully at a later point, it will go a long way toward proving that you are not simply being irresponsible.

To show them you're serious about taking time off, take advantage of every possible resource. Talk to your counselors, your friends, your friends' parents. Get the word out. Every person you talk to will have some new information and insights for you. You may have to argue that paying for a year of college tuition when you don't really want to be there is itself irresponsible. Taking a year off may be the most responsible thing you can do.

The sabbatical tradition grew out of the Judeo-Christian observance of the Sabbath on the seventh day of the week. The day when God rested became a day for people to step away from their work and focus on other things. The Sabbath is designed to rejuvenate and replenish—to bring people back to the rest of the week with a whole new perspective. Taking time off from school can do the same thing for you.

Taking Time Off

Getting Permission

If you're lucky, your parents totally get all of this. But chances are, they probably don't. This is not their fault. Many of them are veterans of the "tune in, turn on, drop out" era where people who took time off either ended up getting drafted to go to Vietnam or volunteered for the *other* army following the Grateful Dead around the country. But many leave-takers, from Tom Brokaw to Alan Greenspan, did come back to the classroom and accomplished great things after they finished their schooling. Others, like Bill Gates and Michael Dell, never did go back to school after their time off, but we doubt their parents have too many complaints.

Perhaps the best argument for taking time off from college is that people who do take a leave get better grades once they return than people who don't, and they get better jobs after graduation. No, we have no study to back this up. But we do know from personal experience that it's true, and we've confirmed it with overwhelming evidence that's emerged from our interviews with students over the years. Since parents have trouble arguing against activities that lead to better grades and better jobs, you should try to pound this truth home when talking to your family about taking time off.

When you think about it, it makes perfect sense. Let's look at the grades side of all of this first. Most eighteen-year-old freshmen arrive at college straight from high school and experience something we call the "Look, Ma, No Hands" syndrome. Cut loose for the first time in their lives with no rules or curfew, the possibilities seem limitless. But many nights each week for months on end, those possibilites amount to little more than drinking a lot, staying up late, and sleeping through class the next day. Not a recipe for a particularly good report card. In essence, many students take their first year off while still paying full tuition.

Colleges don't want your parents to know that this goes on, which is why college tours always take place during the day. But they're so disgusted by it all that they've quietly made it clear that they'd prefer it if you went and did something else for a while after high school before showing up on campus. What, you think we're making this stuff up? Here's the dean of admissions at Harvard talking in *The New York Times*: "Most students would be better off it they were able to get some perspective on themselves, their lives, what they hope to accomplish," he says.[1] Is that not emphatic enough for your folks? How 'bout this gem from Princeton's admissions czar, who once told Ron that "if we wanted to pick precisely the wrong age at which to admit students to college, we have it down pat." Brown University's website encourages all interested students to take time off, Tufts's letter to admitted students encourages them not to come for a year . . . and the list goes on and on.

(All of this encouragement for taking time off raises an interesting question for students who haven't gotten in to college yet: would you be better off taking a year off before you actually *apply*? Possibly. If you're one test score or bad grade short of admission, a year off spent doing something unique and valuable can tip the scales in your favor. Still, there are better ways to position yourself for admission—like studying hard for the SATs in the first place—and your time off will be more enjoyable if you're not spending most of it worrying about your college applications.)

So why are these deans all so sure that taking time off is a good idea? Because they know what both of us proved through experience when we were in college. When you're eighteen years old, you're still fine-tuning your personality. That's a full-time job, particularly when you're away at college and have the freedom to do so without being subject to the

[1] Jodi Wilgoren, "Before College, Year Off Beckons to Well Off," *New York Times*, 17 April 2001, Late edition, sec A, p. 1.

uncomfortable full-time gaze of your parents. There's nothing wrong with this; it's perfectly healthy. But it's hard to do it and concentrate on college at the same time. Ron, at age eighteen, earned gentleman's B's at Amherst. Colin, on the other hand, arrived at Amherst at age twenty with a full head of steam and a burning desire to buckle down in the classroom. He earned mostly A's and graduated magna cum laude. College administrators have seen this over and over, and as far they're concerned, universities would be far better off if their classrooms weren't littered with distracted eighteen year olds.

Taking time off will also be an asset when you do graduate from college. Students often complain that it is difficult to market themselves to potential employers when all they have to show for themselves is a college transcript, a stint on the student council, and a few summer jobs in the mall. But imagine an employer with a stack of one hundred resumes. The first ninety-nine of them come from students who have spent sixteen straight years in school. Then the employer gets to yours, a person who's proven that they're capable of planning a yearlong project and has exhibited maturity and independence. Whose resume would catch your eye?

Time off may also give you an opportunity to investigate some of your career interests. Even if you decide that the line of work you have explored has nothing to do with how you want to spend the rest of your life, you still will have accomplished something very important. But more likely, if you pursue something that interests you, you'll end up being successful and will pursue something similar after you graduate. Ted Conover, one of the people profiled herein, turned his experience during his time off into research for his anthropology thesis. Eventually, he ended up being a best-selling nonfiction author. Tracy Johnston took time off to volunteer for President Clinton's first campaign; later, she went to Oxford as a Rhodes Scholar (just as the president had). Josh Fine was a syndicated radio reporter during his time off, and today he's a producer for *60 Minutes*, the best news show on television. People who take time off end up with great jobs more often than not, and we don't believe that it's just a coincidence.

If the idea of taking time off strikes your parents as something completely outside the norm, they may be surprised to learn that time off is the rule, not the exception, for students in most of the rest of the civilized world. We spoke to several foreign students who were astounded by how anxious American students are to go straight to college and get out as fast as they can. In England, almost all students who study at the university level spend a sabbatical year away from the classroom after they finish secondary school. At one point in 2000, the two most famous college students in the world at the time were both taking time off simultaneously; Prince William spent a year traveling before starting his university studies, and Chelsea Clinton took a semester off to hit the campaign trail with her mother and enjoy one last hurrah at the White House.

The evidence for the value of taking time off is overwhelming, yet your parents may still worry about how it *looks*. There is a certain prestige for them in sending their children to college. They don't want to look as if they've raised a slacker. When the neighbors ask where Susie is going to college, telling them that she is at State U. majoring in business sounds better than trying to explain why she's "dropped out" of school for a while.

Yet these are the same parents who have probably reminded you again and again that they wanted to give you every opportunity in life. Well, the opportunity to go to college is not fleeting. None of these schools are going anywhere. You won't miss anything by not going to college next year. But you might miss out on something great by rushing to college right away. For years, Ben Coolik, another person whose story you'll find in these pages, had dreamed of spending a year after high school in Israel with the friends he'd made during many summers at camp. His father,

Ken, wasn't sure it was a good idea at first, but like any reasonable parent (and most of them are, really!), he eventually came around. "Parents need to be able to analyze their children and their maturity levels," Ken told Ron. "Some people wondered how I could let Ben go, but many more remarked on how wonderful it was that I allowed him to have this experience. They realized how selfish it would have been to keep him closer to my apron strings. It would have been much easier to simply say no."

Thankfully, he didn't. Here's hoping your own parents follow his lead.

But What *Are* You Going to Do?

The best defense is a good offense. So far, we've only been defensive, since there are bound to be at least some people in your life who think that taking time off will turn you into some sort of juvenile delinquent. That is, they will until you convince them that you've got a better idea, something more valuable than being in college for the next year. So what are you going to do, anyway? The answer to that question is your offense. If you can't articulate your reason for staying away from the classroom for a year and how your plan for that year will help you accomplish your goals, you don't deserve to take a sabbatical. "I'll figure it out in September" is not a good enough answer.

Sometimes the most difficult thing to realize is the fact that different options are even available. Your parents and teachers may not have presented you with any possibilities other than going to school for another year. So in our profiles we've tried to paint a precise picture of what those options are, to give you ideas and to prove to your parents that people who take time off can find worthwhile things to do and that they come back to the classroom hungry after their experiences are over.

The question here is not whether an eighteen or twenty year old is qualified to do anything or capable of going somewhere halfway around the world. The real question is, do you want to take charge of your own life or be swept along by everyone else's expectations for you? There's nothing wrong with deciding to go to college; just make sure you're there because *you* want to be.

When to Take Time Off

If you are still in high school, you should go through the college application process, choose a school, and then ask that school to defer your admission until the following year. As we noted above, most colleges will be happy to oblige, and this will be a big relief to your family. It will also take pressure off you, since it's more difficult to apply to college when you are not in school and the resources of your college counselor are not immediately available. If you are in college already when you decide to take your time off, speak to a dean and make sure that a place will be waiting for you when you return.

Some people will warn you that you will be behind your peers when you come back. If they tell you this before you go to college, don't believe them. One year makes little material difference in the broad scheme of things, and the fact that your best friend from high school may graduate from college twelve months earlier than you will seem less significant as time goes by. If they are telling you that you will be behind your peers while you are *in* college, they may have a point. Taking time off after junior year in college and then returning to find all your friends already graduated can be difficult.

Others may warn you about the difficulty of being so far ahead of your new classmates. You may indeed return with more maturity and focus than some of your peers. But why is this bad? The concern is that you will be so much older that you will not be able to relate to your peers. The opposite may in fact be true. During your time off, you will probably be exposed to a broad range of people and experiences. Such exposure can only strengthen your ability to relate to your peers and the other people in your life.

A final warning will be that taking time off is something you should do *after* college. Given that many people graduate with some sort of student loan debt these days, this isn't very practical advice. Besides, one of the best things about taking time off is being able to bring your experiences back to bear on your undergraduate education.

That's why we believe that taking time off *before* graduating from college is ideal. That way, all or part of the incredibly dynamic experience of college will still be in your future, not in your past.

Money

For many, money is the biggest obstacle to taking time off. How much do you have? How much do you need to achieve your goals? How much do you need to have left over when your time off is finished? There are basically three possibilities here: Do you need to make money, break even, or can you spend some money from your savings or family along the way? Because one or both of your parents are probably involved in this issue, you should discuss your financial situation with them at the very beginning of your decision-making process. Your financial status may make taking time off more difficult, but do not, *do not* let it be an insurmountable obstacle. Know your limits, and then find the most creative way to work within them.

Each family's financial situation is different. Your family may have been saving for a long time in preparation for that first college tuition bill. They may also have specific plans to get your brothers and sisters through college. If taking a year off means that tuition payments for you and your sibling or siblings will overlap for an extra year, that may be a problem. On the other hand, that may qualify you for financial aid, or more aid than you would otherwise receive. Also, if you're able to fund your own time off, that multi-thousand-dollar lump that's been sitting in your or your parents' savings account can earn interest during your time off.

College financial aid departments base your aid package on the ability of you and your family to pay tuition. If you have spent some of your savings on taking time off, you may be able to negotiate a more generous financial aid package than you would have before. But your college may also end up asking you to take out a larger loan to make up the difference. If you are on financial aid, speak directly with a dean or an aid officer. Get them to explain all the possible ramifications of your decision to take time off.

Most student loans have a built-in grace period that begins when you leave school. If you take time off, this period may expire, interest will kick in, and you will have to begin making payments. Obviously, it makes sense to plan for this possibility. In some instances, taking a class during your time off (and retaining your status as a student) will postpone the need to begin paying off your loan.

If your only financial need is to break even, there are numerous ways to accomplish this. Some people work for six months to make money and then travel or spend time doing volunteer work. Many opportunities also exist for people who are willing to work for just room and board. You could also try to borrow money interest-free from your parents or another family member. This has obvious advantages; a loan is not so daunting if you can pay it back *after* you have a full-time job.

People who need to save money will probably have to live at home. This issue provokes strong reactions in people. One line of reasoning gocs something like this: Whatever you do during your time off, the absolute worst thing would be to live at home. When you live at home, you sink back into the same old behavior patterns that you spent several years of adolescence attempting to grow out of. Your parents, no doubt, have certain ingrained expectations of who you are, which are based in large part on who you were for so many years. If you are planning to make any positive changes in your life, stay far away from home.

Others believe that living at home is ideal. Some people's parents have always given them the space they needed to be themselves and have encouraged them to be independent. For these people, the benefits of living at home outweigh any loss of freedom that they may feel. Other people get the best of both worlds by finding a friend or relative who will allow them to live in their home rent-free.

Reentry

Reentering school successfully after taking time off is often challenging. Many people find that they have gone through tremendous changes during their time off, and this can make it difficult for them to relate to their friends and family upon their return. Other people are disappointed to discover that their friends are not as interested in hearing about their time off as they had hoped.

Try to keep things in perspective. Remember that many of your friends may be envious that you had the guts to strike off on your own when they did not. Even those who do try to understand your time off may not be able to grasp all the changes that you've experienced. They may still look at you as though you're the same person you were when you left. The ultimate test of the worth of your time off may well be your ability to integrate the new things that you learned into an environment that probably didn't change much while you were away.

Part 1

Work

Kristin Erickson
BROWN UNIVERSITY
Worked for a nursing service in Appalachia and on an
organic farm

As she approached her senior year at Brearley, a small, private girls' school in New York City, Kristin didn't know where she wanted to go to college, or even if she wanted to go at all. Her parents, meanwhile, had aspirations of their own. "They made me look at schools like Harvard. I think that was because both of them grew up in small towns and had never had that kind of opportunity. This was *their* chance to go to Harvard."

When Kristin raised the idea of taking time off, "My parents freaked out a little bit," she said. "Ultimately they said, 'Okay, but you have to have a complete plan.'"

Eventually she came up with one: working as a courier for the Frontier Nursing Service in rural Appalachia. Founded in 1925, FNS is a health-care organization in Kentucky with a hospital and other outpost clinics. Originally, doctors visited the more remote areas on horseback. The mail took a long time to get there, and FNS volunteer couriers would bring mail to all the clinics. They still need people to deliver mail, and today's volunteers also help out with many other chores.

The application process was easy and straightforward, and FNS offered Kristin a spot. She left for Kentucky during the summer after high school, even though some New York friends were skeptical. "Oh, Appalachia," she remembers them saying. "Better bring your own toilet paper."

Kristin joined ten other couriers, aged seventeen and up, who were volunteering at FNS in exchange for room and board.

"I started going on home health rounds once a week. This woman, Maybelline, and I would spend the day driving around to people's homes. We bathed homebound patients who couldn't bathe themselves because they were old or disabled. Growing up in New York City, I saw a lot of intense, crazy things. But there was something very intimate about going into someone's home and bathing their body. There was a lot of trust involved in that.

"I gave a bath to this frail little guy married to a big-mama woman. He must have been ninety years old. They had something like sixteen kids together. One time we were walking, and he points to his crotch and says, 'See that? Sixteen kids.' He was fantastic.

"You had to get to certain people every day, but there were days with fewer patients, so it never felt rushed. Sometimes you'd just end up sitting around drinking coffee and hanging out with a family.

"It could also be very depressing. In one home, the daughter went to work every day in nice clothes, but the house was just crazy. When it was sprayed, they collected a five-pound bag of cockroaches."

Kristin spent a lot of her time just listening. "When I graduated from high school, I had all these fixed ideas about how I felt about this and what to do about that. And when I got to Kentucky, I just shut my mouth and listened. A lot of my organized high school ideas were tossed around and smashed. Which was great, but it was also confusing."

One of Kristin's favorite people was Sherman, an eighty-three-year-old craftsman who taught her how to build furniture out of walnut wood. "I used to go over to his house at six in the morning. We'd drink coffee and shoot the shit. I built a rocking chair with him. He'd always say, 'Women is the cause of all trouble.' And I'd say, 'Sherman, men is the cause of all trouble, and you know it.'"

Kristin was at FNS through December, and she decided that she wanted to stay on. "I had been through enough compartmentalized experiences in my life. I didn't want to just up and go right when I was really getting into it."

Kristin continued to involve herself in a variety of projects. "I became friends with a woman named Lucile—everyone called her Thumper. She was a thirty-year FNS veteran and had started to lose her vision. She wanted to reread *Pilgrim's Progress,* but her eyes were all screwy. So I said, 'I'll read it to you,' which became a really fun thing to do."

Kristin's plan for the second half of her time off was to work on a farm in Pennsylvania. "I got room, board, and a small weekly stipend in return for working six days a week for ten or twelve hours a day at the farm. I was living in a barn, and my geography became pretty local while I was there. I worked with four other apprentices like myself."

The farm grew all kinds of vegetables and sold them to upscale markets and fancy restaurants in Philadelphia.

"One time, we all went into Philadelphia after a day of work and ate at one of the restaurants. Here we are, all of us with dirt under our fingernails and in the cracks of our skin no matter how hard we scrubbed: 'Yes, please, I'd like the special salad this evening.' And there were all these vegetables, beautifully arranged on the plate, which we had been cutting by the handful that afternoon, with a massive price on it. It was wild."

Kristin's schedule had a fair amount of regularity to it, since the farm had two delivery days per week. Of the four remaining workdays, two were for harvesting the crops for the next day's orders. "First thing in the morning, we'd go out and cut chives. Chives are all perky in the morning when they have dew on them, but later in the day they lose their moisture and get kind of limp.

"There was always way more work than we could possibly do. Sometimes there was something to be done and it would be Sunday, our day off. But plants don't observe Sundays. So instead of baking my bread for the week, doing laundry, and lying by the creek, I would go out and do it.

"There is an incredible satisfaction that comes from working so hard physically on something and then *seeing* it. Once, at the end of a long day, we were all tired and the sun was going down. And there were 2,000 tomato plants left unplanted. 'But dammit,' we said, 'we were supposed to do it today, and those really should get into the ground. They're getting really big. Let's do it. Let's just load them up and go out to the field.'

"And we just did it. Plant and plant and plant, and the sun goes down and you're still planting, planting, and then stop, and they're there: beautiful rows of tomato plants."

Kristin spent a lot of time alone in Pennsylvania. "It was solitude but not loneliness. After a long day, I didn't want to talk with anybody. I just wanted to make food, write a few sentences in my journal, and crash. It was a very focused time. My only goal was to write something every day in my journal. Sometimes the only entry would be 'Picked 100 quarts of strawberries today.' Then I'd pass out.

"I have a couple entries that just say 'Rain!' Sometimes people would come to the farm on a sunny day in the middle of a long dry spell and say, 'What a beautiful day.' We thought, 'Oh, yeah, beautiful day, everything's dying. It's great.' Rain was a godsend at times."

Kristin learned a lot from Mark, the farm's owner, who had taught agriculture in college for eighteen years. She felt she was "making up for a deficit of eighteen years spent living in a city. I was like a little kid running around asking questions. I feel lucky that Mark was so willing to answer my questions."

Kristin left the farm at the end of the summer, in time to start Brown University. "It was hard to leave. I almost decided to stay through the harvest. When I was planning it, I thought, 'Oh, four months, what a nice long time to be on a farm.' But four months is nothing."

Leaving the farm reminded Kristin of a unicorn tapestry at the Cloisters, the medieval museum back in New York. "Of course, in the tapestry, all the plants are flowering at once. But the only way to see all the plants and flowers blossom in the garden is to spend four seasons there. My advice is, if you're going to be on a farm, be there for the whole year. No question. I didn't harvest what I planted, and that made me feel something was very incomplete."

The college environment seemed "ludicrous" to Kristin when she first arrived. "I got the course catalog, and looking through it, I saw courses in women's studies. I thought, 'Where's the men's studies department? What's going on here?'

"College feels to me like a very soft, cushy, and in some ways irresponsible environment. So much intellectualizing. An old teacher of mine was telling me to join all these various feminist organizations. I said, 'All I can control is myself. I'm in charge of myself, and I'm a woman.' I felt very strong and all the organizations seemed so far removed from the real world. I think my approach to things like that has become much more personal and less formulaic."

Kristin did find one course in the catalog that she was excited about: "Plants, Food, and People. It was plant biology and agriculture. My little academic harvesting."

Socially, Kristin made friends almost by accident. "When people first come to college, there is a whole mentality of 'Oh, God, I have to have this intense camp experience. Let's all be best friends right now, this week.' Because we're all so unsure of ourselves.

"I didn't really throw myself into dorm life. I would just take off on my bike early in the morning and do my own thing. But in not looking for people, I collided with some remarkable folks.

"The things that interest me most are always underneath the surface. It takes a while to find that out, as in a relationship with someone. It could take a year to get past all that initial stuff. It's like digging down into the soil. There's so much going on, and you just keep seeing more."

For more information . . .

www.frontiernursing.org—Frontier Nursing Service couriers live in rural Appalachia and perform home health-care rounds with traveling nurses. Couriers also do chores and assorted grunt work in and around the FNS clinic in Wendover, Kentucky. Room and board are provided. (606) 672-2318.

Integrating Community Service into Nursing Education: A Guide to Service-Learning, by Patricia A. Bailey, Dona Rinaldi, and Patricia Harrington; Springer Publishing Company, Inc.; 1999. Written by nurse educators, this book provides a guide to applying service learning to the nursing curriculum.

Barzella Estle
UNIVERSITY OF ALABAMA
Worked as a model

Barzella Estle's high school class in Saraland, Alabama, a suburb fifteen miles outside Mobile, graduated 250 kids. After high school, almost half of them got married, half went to community colleges, and a few went directly to four-year colleges. Barzella, however, ended up in the pages of *Seventeen.*

"I had never taken people seriously before when they told me I should model. My best friend in high school, Ava, she was captain of the dance line, and all the guys were always like, 'Oooh, Ava, she's so hot.' No one ever gave me a second look.

"It's like a big joke when I go home now. One time, some guys came over, and they said, 'Barzella, why didn't you ever go out in high school?' And my mom says right back to them, 'Well, hell, no one ever asked her.'"

During her senior year in high school, Barzella worked for Gayfers, a local department store. "It was my sister's second husband who finally convinced me to ask them if I could try modeling for them. My boss, who was the public relations director for the store, liked me a lot. She ended up using me for local newspaper ads and then I ended up in the ad in the back-to-school issue of *Seventeen.*

"It boosted my self-confidence a lot. I thought maybe I just had something going for me that no one else had noticed yet."

Barzella was so preoccupied with going to college that she didn't seriously consider the possibility of modeling full-time. "In Alabama, college football is a religion, and I grew up loving the University of

Alabama Crimson Tide. I got scholarship offers from smaller schools, but it was either Alabama or bust," she said.

When Barzella arrived in Tuscaloosa, however, she found that there was much more to school than the Saturday game. "It's a very Greek-oriented school. If you're not in a fraternity or a sorority, you're not anything. So I went through rush, but I just wasn't from the right family. None of the good sororities picked me up. No one knew who I was."

Barzella made the best of it and pledged one of the newest sororities on campus. "The money part was ridiculous. They fined you for missing chapter meetings or not wearing your Greek letters on Friday. It costs more to pay house dues and be in a sorority at Alabama than it does to pay tuition. I de-pledged after two months, and I was an instant nonperson. I felt like such a huge outcast. All the rich girls and pretty girls were here or there, and I just didn't fit in," she said.

To make matters worse, Barzella was also struggling academically. "I had no idea what I was in for. I kept my nose in the books in high school, but the public-school system in Alabama just isn't very good, and I was not prepared at all. I basically just paddled through my classes, and I didn't get above a 2.5 my first three semesters," she said.

Before she even had a chance to transfer, however, she had a lucky break. "After my senior year in high school, *Model* magazine was holding a cover-girl contest, so I sent a few pictures in and didn't think anything of it," she explained.

"Right after my first set of finals in December of my freshman year, I was in the grocery store with my roommates, and they had *Model* in the magazine rack. The cover had a teaser about the cover-girl finalists, and I opened it up and said, 'Oh, my God!' My girlfriend, she just started screaming, 'That's you, that's you!' They had never called to tell me.

"I didn't win, but that really sparked my interest. The bug had hit me, and I wanted to see what I could do with it. I found a woman who ran a small modeling agency in Birmingham, and the summer after my freshman year she took me to a national modeling convention. It turned out that a new New York agency that had been profiled in *Model* in the same issue that I was in was at the convention. They remembered me and signed me up," she said.

By then Barzella already had registered to begin her sophomore year, so she agreed to move to New York City at the end of the semester. "I went back to school, and I shouldn't have. I didn't care about anything except getting the hell out of Alabama. I did so horribly that semester; I was so ashamed. I should have filed for academic bankruptcy," she said.

When winter finally arrived, Barzella bought a one-way Amtrak ticket to New York City. "I didn't think twice about what it meant to move to New York. I had my two footlockers and my jam box, and off I went.

"My agency didn't have an apartment for the models, so they had set me up with a room at a Salvation Army all-women boardinghouse. It was real secure, and it was good for my transition. Later on, I ended up moving into an apartment with someone I met through work," she said.

Barzella visited her new agency the day after her arrival, and they already had arranged a number of auditions for her. Since she didn't have any idea where any of them were, she decided it would be best to learn the city methodically first.

"I studied the map for three days. I studied the subway, the building numbers, and which way the traffic went, so I could look nonchalant, like I knew where I was going," she said.

Even though she had planned to do print work only, she found her way to an audition for a Heineken commercial. "It ended up being my first job. We filmed it at night on the Brooklyn Bridge. It was in January, and it was so cold. It took seven hours," she said.

As if she needed any further evidence that the workday of a New York model isn't all glitz and glamour, the grueling audition process drove it home. "They would examine you from head to toe. Some of them would make you put on a bathing suit and come out and turn around. Others would measure every part of your body and then take Polaroids.

"I hated being on the spot. One day I was out running errands, just in grubby clothes or whatever, and I stopped by my agency to pick up a check. My agent said, 'You know, Barzella, you really need to work on your appearance.' I was always on display."

The scoldings that Barzella received from her agent were a not-so-gentle reminder that she was a bit out of her element, but she tried not to let it bother her. "It was like going to Mars. When I first moved there, no one could understand me because I talked so fast and my accent was so Southern. I made an idiot of myself on many occasions, with the wrong attire, or not having the proper manners, or just blurting out the wrong English," she said.

She took comfort in the fact that she was not the only model in New York to have been plucked out of a small town. "One of my best friends there came from Shinglehouse, Pennsylvania. She's now married to a power broker and living in a fancy apartment on the Upper East Side. Her husband is sending her to cooking school," she added.

"It was kind of nice, actually. The agency sometimes would take all the girls out to dinner, and they would have agency parties. It was kind of like the sorority I never got into at Alabama. I had no problem making friends in New York."

Though the work wasn't steady at first, by the end of the spring it began to pick up. "Eventually, I was working at least once a week. I did *Glamour*,

Mademoiselle, and a shoot for *Woman's World,* where they made me look like I was about thirty. Then there was this one where I was in a wedding gown. I told my mom to buy twenty copies of that one because it was the last time she would ever see me in a wedding dress!"

The pay was generally excellent, but Barzella soon discovered that there was an inverse relationship between the size of her check and the prestige of the job. "The bridal thing paid $1,500 for four hours, and when you would work in a showroom trying on new clothes for reps from department stores, you'd make about $150 an hour. But *Glamour* paid like $150 a day, because girls would kill to do that," she said.

Sometimes, however, even the best payday wasn't worth what she had to put up with. "There were a lot of slimeballs trying to get a little too cozy after the shoot. I would finally get comfortable with a photographer, but when they make a pass at you, it just ruins the chemistry," she said.

Barzella became friends with the owner of a restaurant on the Upper East Side, and she decided to take job as a hostess to have more of a regular cash flow. The restaurant, it turned out, was a hangout for all sorts of interesting characters.

"I got to know one of New York's crime families pretty well. One of the big guys in the family kind of liked me, and he invited me to their Christmas party. They had covered up the windows of the restaurant with fake snow so that the federal agents outside could not see who was inside," she said.

"I also ran the music at night at the restaurant. Two guys from Miami were there one night, and they were starting a party called Disco Inferno at the Roxy, this great club. They asked me if I wanted to learn how to work a real turntable, and the next thing I knew I was the DJ at their party.

"So, by then, I was studying at the Actors Institute on Monday nights, going out on casting calls and modeling during the day, working at the restaurant on other nights, and working at the Roxy till 5 A.M. on Fridays. Then on Saturday I'd watch college football. I wouldn't even answer the phone. I had to see how Alabama was doing," she said.

Alabama, it turned out, was equally concerned with how Barzella was doing. Her mother and stepfather, who had never been to New York, drove up to see her. "I ended up getting booked the days they were here. I left them maps and directions and everything, but I don't think they went outside the apartment once without me. They were petrified.

"I had an uncle come to visit me, and he said, 'Now, you're not doing drugs or anything, are you, Barzella?' All my family, they prayed for me at night. I think they thought I had gone off on the wrong track. They couldn't really comprehend the life I was leading."

It seemed that life couldn't get any crazier, until Barzella began her affair with a prominent former NFL football player. "A sportscaster who hung out at the restaurant introduced me to him, and we ended up being involved for two years. He was still kind of married when we started dating, but they had been having problems for a while."

After almost two years, the pace began to wear on Barzella, and she began to think about going back to school. "I investigated New York University, but my grades were too low to get in there or anyplace else, really. Alabama was so cheap, and my parents wanted me to come back because they knew I was going to lose my residency status. So I decided to go back," she said.

Not before she talked it over with a few of her trusted advisors, however. "O. J. Simpson used to hang out at the restaurant a lot. When I told him I was going to go to school again, he told me I was going backward and making a huge mistake. He kept saying, 'You don't go from Alabama to New York back to Alabama! You go from Alabama to New York to L.A.'"

After two years in New York City, returning to Tuscaloosa was a letdown. "Being stuck there with all these frat-daddies and sorority girls—I guess I did have some readjustment problems," she said.

Barzella coped by throwing herself into her academic work. "Being in New York, I saw a lot of B.S. It finally hit me that I wasn't really all that aware of what was going on around me. I was so caught up in modeling and the fast-paced jet-setting that academically I was, well, not dumb, but just behind," she said.

She also discovered some hidden talents. "Originally I was going to major in public relations. That's what my boss had done at Gayfers, and I liked her job. So I was taking mass communications, and in the lab we had a lot of writing to do. I found out that I had a knack for writing in the journalistic style, and all of a sudden I was making A's. I started volunteering for the school newspaper, and eventually I got paid jobs working for the university."

Though not everyone has the looks for modeling, a large number of high school students have talents of their own that they've always dreamed about pursuing full-time. Maybe it's a season or two of minor league baseball or a year with a ballet company in a small city.

Barzella encourages anyone with raw talent—whatever the field—to take a year off and reach for the stars. "The best way to grow is to try and pursue something like that. I pictured myself sitting in a rocking chair when I was eighty years old, reflecting back on my life, and I didn't want to regret not having done something. I wasn't a wild success story, but I was able to go up there and send some money home to my parents and buy a car and pay for some of my tuition. I wouldn't discourage anyone from my background from trying to do the same thing," she said.

Since graduation, Barzella has stuck with publishing. She's spent several years working for various divisions of AOL Time Warner. And she finally did put on a wedding dress again. Today, she's taking time off once more to raise two children, though she plans on working full-time again once they're in school. In the meantime, she edits cookbooks on a freelance basis and even does some modeling from time to time.

"I'm extremely lucky in the sense that I've been able to build upon every decision I've ever made. Taking my time off during college was still one of the best decisions I've ever made. Living in a college town [Gainesville], I meet so many kids who are graduating and have no clue what they want to do. They choose majors because they're easy or sound cool, yet they have not matured enough to know the sacrifice involved with having a career. I would highly recommend someone taking time off or at least getting work experience during the summers. Don't feel rushed to graduate in four years!

"My husband and I have very different opinions about this. I think mostly because of our college experience. He was in a situation [with the] navy where he was forced to finish in four years. However, he was set with a job in the mavy upon graduating. For the rest of the people in the world who are not so fortunate, you should seriously evaluate what you're doing and get the experience while you're young and can do so."

For more information . . .

www.newfaces.com—Offers links to national/international modeling agencies, talent agencies, modeling jobs, magazines, calendars, and many other modeling sites.

www.modelnetwork.com—"The modeling industry online." Exactly.

www.cosmoworlds.com—Offers links to national/international modeling agencies.

Josh Fine
UNIVERSITY OF MICHIGAN
Created a one-man radio network to cover the first
Clinton campaign for college radio stations

The lightbulbs started going off in Josh Fine's head as he strolled down 34th Street in New York City during the summer of 1992.

Josh was working at the Democratic National Convention. He spent much of his time running errands as a page for the Democratic National Committee, but he also did some reporting for the radio station at the University of Michigan.

"I was walking from DNC headquarters to Madison Square Garden, and I started thinking about all the reporters who were there from all over the world," he recalled. "Issues kept coming up that directly related to college students, but no cohesive group of college reporters was there to interpret them.

"I had been keeping a journal of everything I observed at the convention. My roommate was always asleep, so I would go down to the hotel bar to write. That night I just sat there for hours, spitting out all these ideas."

When he returned home to Chicago a few days later, he sat his father down for a talk. "I told him that I had this crazy idea: to take time off to build a network of college radio stations to cover the presidential campaign. I told him that I would need to raise a lot of money, find stations to carry the reports, and a bunch of other things. I knew there was not a lot of time to pull it together.

"My father suggested I talk to some people in the media business about it. He actually never had a problem with the idea of my taking time off, as long as it was to do something moderately productive."

Josh approached a few industry types, and they were excited. "They were clear that it could, that it *needed* to happen, so after that I knew it was at least a possibility," he said.

An executive at NBC in Chicago whom Josh had met through a summer internship was his most helpful advisor. She walked him through the long list of logistical issues he would need to address to set up a one-man network in less than six weeks.

"She was amazing. She knew exactly what it would cost, what I needed to do technically, that I had to target stations in swing states, where the student votes would really matter—so the campaign would take me seriously," he said. "Never in my wildest dreams would I have been able to put all that together in my head."

The technical aspects of building the network were easy enough. Josh found a company that gave him a free voice-mail box, so he could call in every day and record his reports for the client stations to retrieve on their own.

But he soon realized how difficult it was going to be to finance the operation. "At first, we figured I would need $50,000 to finance the project, but we eventually lowered that number dramatically. We quickly found out that there is no money in college radio. We were hoping to get 100 stations to pay $300 each. Many stations were interested, but few of them could pay. We ended up giving the reports away to several stations," he said.

Josh went to foundations, corporate sponsors, and many individuals for financial support, and was turned away regularly. "It became clear that this was not the way to go," Josh recalled. "As curious as people seemed to be, no one wanted to touch anything that looked at all political."

Eventually Josh tapped into a nationwide network of voter-education projects. Bit by bit, tiny grant by tiny grant, he collected enough to finance his first few weeks on the road.

Josh knew that he would need to spend about 75 percent of his time with Bill Clinton, since Clinton seemed to spend much more time addressing issues that concerned college students than Bush did. His final task was getting a seat on the Clinton campaign plane. "I had to push hard for that, but I was definitely the right reporter at the right time," he explained. "They were targeting the youth vote, and I came in with a large number of potential listeners." He told the campaign that he would start around Labor Day.

As his departure date drew near, Josh still did not have enough money to stay on the road through Election Day. "I had about $7,500, nowhere near enough money to finish. I thought maybe I should just say, 'Hey, I gave it my best shot, but it didn't turn out the way that I wanted and life goes on,'" he recalled.

"But my dad said to go, that once I was actually out there making it happen and getting some publicity, it would be easier to raise the money. And if worse came to worst, I would come home at the end of September.

"Shortly before I left to join the campaign, I stayed up talking with a friend almost all night. She told me, 'You could regret not going, but you'll never regret having given it your best shot.'"

So Josh left a few days later with a mental list of the issues that he wanted to cover. "A lot of issues in this campaign had a specific bearing on young people's lives," he said. "Some of them, like the national debt, had gotten a lot of play in the national press. But others, like the environment and the economics of national service, were really almost untouched by the media as a whole."

Josh flew to Portland, Oregon, just as his friends were returning to Ann Arbor. "Their reaction was a mix of 'You're crazy' and 'That's the greatest idea I've ever heard,'" he recalled. "I knew I would miss being in school, but I never really minded taking the semester off. I knew there was just no other way to do it."

When Josh got off the plane, he lugged his bags to the first rally of the day and was greeted by pandemonium. "It was the biggest trip ever," he said. "There were people screaming 'Traveling press, traveling press,' and I remember thinking, 'Oh, they must mean me.'

"They treated us like royalty. I was on these planes and buses with people like Gwen Ifill from *The New York Times* [now of *Washington Week*] and Mara Liasson from National Public Radio. I was completely starry-eyed." That first day, Josh traveled to Eugene, Oregon, where he reported on an environmental rally. Later that day, he took his first ride on the press plane to San Francisco.

"They called the press plane the zoo plane, and it was the greatest thing ever," Josh said. "I learned more on that plane with those 150 reporters than anywhere else. It *was* kind of like a zoo—a giant traveling fraternity—with streamers everywhere and food and beer. God, those are really the best memories I have.

"I had hoped the whole experience would be fun, but I didn't expect it to be. I thought it would be really lonely, out in random cities with reporters who were all older, who would not give a shit about me, sitting in hotel rooms by myself and working really hard."

Instead Josh was surprised at how quickly people took to him. "I think they were excited by what I was doing and excited to have a young person around," he said. "I was amazed by the friendliness of it all."

Meanwhile, friends at home were seeking additional financial support on his behalf, and Josh said that the other reporters also helped him out.

"They've all got these basically unlimited expense accounts, so they were really nice about picking up the tab when we went out or letting me crash in their rooms if there was an extra bed," he said.

Josh found other ways to save as well. He flew commercial flights at times, since paying for a seat on the campaign plane cost more than first class on an airline. He stayed with friends when he could and managed to stay in Chicago for a few weekends as well.

Though Josh ended up spending about 80 percent of his time with Clinton, he spent enough time with Bush to see how markedly different their campaigns were. "I did a whole story one day on the music they played at their campaign stops. Bush played presidential-march-type music, and Clinton played Arrested Development. You get the idea," he said.

Josh filed at least one story to his voice-mail box each day, often focusing on a speech the candidate had made. "I tried to focus on a particular speech or appearance and then have a representative from the opposing candidate sound-biting their response. That way, I didn't get any complaints about balance," he said.

Josh said that his best moments professionally came when he asked questions that the candidates were not expecting. "I was at a press conference where a high-level admiral from the Reagan/Bush years announced his endorsement of Clinton. It was pretty civil," he recalled.

Civil, that is, until the admiral stunned the room into silence by answering Josh's question about Clinton's plan to allow gays in the military. "He said he didn't agree at all, but that he was sure Clinton was open-minded enough to consider all sides of that issue," Josh recalled. "That was my proudest moment. All these veteran reporters came up to me afterward and said that that was the best question of the news conference. It was one of my best stories of the campaign, because it was my voice actually asking the question."

Josh also landed a very brief one-on-one interview with Clinton a few days before the election. Clinton was backstage at the Meadowlands in East Rutherford, New Jersey, when Campaign Press Secretary Dee Dee Myers sent an aide to bring Josh, who had been clamoring for a one-on-one for several weeks, to the holding area where Clinton was waiting to make a speech.

"'Okay, Josh, now's your chance,' she told me. 'You get one question.' I had about five minutes to decide, to think about the one issue that was on the minds of all young people," he said.

"I finally decided on national service, an idea that got huge applause at every stop, and I think it's safe to say was a total fraud," he said. "Clinton was essentially saying that everyone could pay for college by working for two years, which was not at all what ended up being submitted to Congress."

Josh did not want to push him too hard, however. "That's one of the most disappointing things I learned about the whole process. You have to ask your questions in only a moderately challenging way, because if you don't, you lose access altogether," he said. Clinton told Josh that he thought his promises were fair and his proposals were financially feasible. He eventually proposed to start AmeriCorps, a program that would include 70,000 participants by 1997. It still exists today.

As the campaign wound down, Josh made plans to be in Little Rock for the victory celebration. After a few days of covering meetings on the transition, he returned to Chicago to wait for the second semester of school to begin.

"I was absolutely thrilled to go back to school," he said. "It was so nice to be somewhere where my only job was to do my homework, and everyone was my own age again. It was refreshing after spending all my time with thirty- and forty-year-olds for three months."

Though Josh missed the adrenaline surge from the daily reporting grind, his experiences helped him develop a different attitude about school. "I learned that these people in my field, the top people, most of them did go to college, but they can't remember what they took, got poor grades in the classes they can remember, and didn't necessarily go to good schools in the first place," he said. "My new attitude was basically that I would take full advantage of the things that really interested me, and those that didn't, I just wouldn't worry about."

Back in school, Josh put his journalism skills to work by hosting a weekly political talk show called *By the People*. He also worked as the sports director for the university's radio station. After graduating as a political science major in May 1995, Josh went to work for one of the first online news services and eventually covered the 1996 campaign as well. Josh agreed that it might seem intimidating for anyone to try to reproduce what he did in future campaigns. But he insisted that it's not out of reach for most college students with some radio experience. "It was just a question of drive, having the will to stay up until four in the morning faxing things off and making it happen. It took a lot of chutzpah, but it was not a smarts kind of thing. I didn't have any more smarts than anyone else."

His employers since then might beg to differ. Because he had achieved one very significant first—becoming the first college student to cover a presidential campaign full-time—MSNBC had enough confidence to hire him to blaze another trail, as one of the first correspondents to cover a campaign on a website. "Pretty much everything flows from that time off," Josh said. "My life would unquestionably have been totally different without it."

After working his way through several lower-level jobs in New York City, Josh eventually landed one of the best journalism jobs on the planet: today he's an associate producer for Mike Wallace on CBS News's *60 Minutes.*

For more information . . .

www.politicsonline.com — "Fundraising & Internet Tools for Politics" site offering many links to political coverage of the presidential elections, campaigns, candidates, parties, statistics, and webcasts.

www.politics1.com — "The Most Comprehensive Online Guide to American Politics, Candidates, & Parties" website offering exactly what www.politicsonline.com does.

www.radio-locator.com — Online search engine for national and international radio stations.

www.radio-directory.fm — "Listen to the radio on the Web." Provides Web radio links and radio directory, all for free.

www.current.org/radio — Provides public radio links, public webcasts, and brief descriptions of radio stations.

www.geocities.com/mike_reilley_2000/newswriting/ accolades.html — "The Journalist's Toolbox" offers more than 11,000 online resources for editors, reporters, and news librarians.

Political Campaign Communication: Inside and Out, by Larry Powell. Allyn & Bacon, 2002. Examination of the ins and outs of political campaigning from the perspective of an academic/political consultant.

The Little Book of Campaign Etiquette: For Everyone with a Stake in Politicians and Journalists, by Stephen Hess. Brookings Institution Press, 2000. Offers broad coverage of campaign-related topics, with suggestions, illustrations, how-tos, and how-to-nots.

Campaigns and Conscience, by Phillip M. Seib. Greenwood Publishing, 1994. Covers ethical topics of the relationship between journalists and politicians and provides an inside look into how reporters and candidates get things done.

Toni Gorog
UNIVERSITY OF CALIFORNIA AT BERKELEY
Worked with scientists in the rain forests of Brazil

Toni Gorog's infectious enthusiasm for science can catch people off guard. Even Toni was not fully prepared for how far, literally, her passion could take her.

After graduating from high school in Princeton, New Jersey, Toni lived at home during the summer and fall while working at a deli. In January 1990, she left for the University of California at Berkeley to begin college.

"Academically speaking, Berkeley was difficult. I had registered biology as my area of interest and was following their guidelines for course selection. I quickly learned what studying hard means."

In the fall of 1992, Toni finished what she called "those pain-in-the-butt lower-division courses full of pre-meds" that she was required to take. "It's stressful to be in a classroom with 600 students where the competition is cutthroat. I was relieved to get into the upper-division classes specific to my major. There were some amazing and energetic professors who made those classes more interesting.

"My first good upper-division class was Comparative Animal Physiology. Then in the spring of 1993 I took the class that opened up a whole world of possibilities for me: Natural History of the Vertebrates. We studied birds, mammals, and reptiles and amphibians. During our in-class lab we learned, by looking at animals and memorizing, how to tell different species apart, what they eat, where they live, and when they migrate. We also had field lab once a week. It was great, because we actually got to see the Bay Area and visit different parks."

During the mammology section, the class did some live trapping. "The traps we used didn't hurt the animals. They walked in to get the bait, triggered a spring, and the door closed, so they were stuck inside. We then took the animal out and performed all the measurements, like weight, body length, ear length, and tail length. We also learned how to identify California species."

Toni's enthusiasm did not go unnoticed. "I would go out there all the time with my friend Rachel, who was also a student in the class. Sometimes we wouldn't take notes. We would just sit and watch the birds we were studying, because it was so fun. We started to get to know our TA, Albert, a grad student from Brazil who was working on his Ph.D."

Albert told Toni of his plans to return to Brazil the next summer to do fieldwork for his dissertation on fruit bats. "I talked with Rachel and we said to ourselves, 'Fieldwork in Brazil could be amazing. Let's ask Albert if he wants our help.'

"One day we were hanging out with him at the end of a lab, and we said to him, 'By the way, do you think you would ever need any help?' Albert's response was 'Oh, I don't know, maybe.' A few weeks later, Albert came up to us and said, 'You know, I've been thinking about what you said, and I am going to need some help. If you want to, you can come.' We were stunned. We thought, 'No, it's not going to happen.' But it did.

"It turned out that Albert needed help during the following fall semester. I decided, 'This experience will be so worthwhile. I'm going to go.' I owe it all to that class. I know that sounds cheesy, but it's true. There are well-known biologists who credit this class when they publish their papers: 'Yeah, I took IB 104 ten years ago, and it's the reason I'm a biologist now.'"

Albert's advisor had another Brazilian grad student, Meika, who was also going back to Brazil at the same time to do her fieldwork. "So he asked us, 'Any chance that you want to help Meika, also?' And we said, 'Sure, fine. You arrange it, we'll do it.' We sat and planned with Meika and Albert. But a lot of things were left unplanned. We weren't really sure exactly what was going to be happening in Brazil."

Toni was responsible only for her round-trip airfare, which she paid for out of her savings from previous jobs. Albert and Meika took care of all other essentials. "I didn't even borrow money from my parents, who supported the idea. They weren't worried that I was going to flake off and never come back to school. My friends were also excited for me.

"Rachel, Albert, Meika, and I met in Sao Paulo, Brazil, on September 1. Three of us took a bus to Parani to pick up our car, a 1979 VW Bug. We would be driving along, come up over a hill, and find a huge bus in our lane barreling toward us. When Rachel came back to the U.S., she immediately got a ticket for driving too close behind someone else, because in Brazil you just follow right on their tail. It doesn't matter; there are no rules.

"We did so much driving because the areas of primary forest are few and far between. Minas Gerais, a state in eastern Brazil, looked totally deforested. It was really sad."

There was no such thing as a typical day for Toni and her group. "Albert and Meika were doing similar research. They were trying to understand the diversification of species and explain the fragmentation of different groups of animals in the rain forest. The basic purpose of the project was to look at the geographical distribution of species and populations in order to uncover the history of the groups and the forests in which they lived. Studying those basic patterns lays a foundation for the sound management of biological diversity."

Albert was studying several groups of tropical fruit bats. "We were catching the bats with Japanese mist nets. People also use them for catching birds. You can stretch out the nets between trees or poles. They come in different lengths and they're about three to four meters [ten to thirteen feet] high. They're made of really fine thread, and have little looped-down pockets. So if an animal flies into the net, it will drop into the pocket and get tangled up in it."

Meika was researching a group of small marsupials known as the mouse opossum, or *Marmosops*. "She was carrying 120 traps—eighty Shermans and forty Tomahawks. Shermans are made of either steel or aluminum. Tomahawks are bigger and they're made of wire. They are both live traps.

"Our objective was to collect tissue samples from the animals they were studying. Those samples were then brought back to be housed in a museum. Researchers can sequence parts of the DNA to study evolutionary relationships between groups of animals and can infer how long ago the divisions between them occurred.

"It was necessary to keep really good records of the localities we worked in and the measurements we took. I was constantly writing things down and taking notes. Our notes were bound and put into the museum collection for anyone who wants to use our work."

Toni's group traveled all around southeastern Brazil. "We'd usually arrive wherever we were going sometime in the afternoon. At about six in the evening, we would go and set out the mist nets. We couldn't open them before it was dark because then we'd end up catching birds instead of bats. We'd mist-net until about midnight, sometimes until one. And then we'd take the nets down and go to bed.

"We would usually wake up around seven, and if we had already set up Meika's traps, we would go out and check them. If not, we would go out and set them. We baited the traps with peanut butter and bananas.

"Usually, the first day there wouldn't be that much work. If we hadn't had time to mist-net the night before, we wouldn't have any samples to prepare, so we'd have some free time in the afternoon.

"First we would measure the animal. Each bat gets a tag, from which you can tell species, sex, all the measurements we took, the locality, the altitude at which it was caught, the name of the collector, and the name of the person who prepared the specimen. The specimens are invaluable. They provide important information about reproduction, distribution, genetics, and morphology that is fundamental for conservation programs.

"It was hard even to find time to write in my journal, but I managed to do it. Luckily there were a few times when we'd go on a hike to a waterfall and swim."

Toni worked in Brazil from September to December 1993, and says she fell in love with the country. "Everywhere we went, I would say, 'Okay, you guys go on, I'm going to stay here.' I had just read Garcia Marquez's *One Hundred Years of Solitude*. One afternoon I came to a house that used to border a coffee plantation that had since vanished. It was just like the Buendiases' house in the novel. I took a shower in a bathroom with huge windows facing this overflowing garden fading into a forest of purple flowers."

Toni got along well with her companions. She also said the trip was an important confidence builder for her. "I have field experience that many grad students don't have. It's nice to be able to talk about what I've done and be able to understand what other people have been through. I never regretted devoting myself to school before, but after this experience, there was just no question that I was completely into my studies.

"I used to get really caught up in school and in trying to do well. I would get bummed out when my grades weren't ideal. Now, having done this, I feel I might be good at what I do. I also know that being good at something isn't only a question of grades." Toni has since graduated from Berkeley and is pursuing a Ph.D. in biology at the University of Michigan.

"If you want to do field research, the best thing is go around and talk to people. If there is someone who inspires you, go and talk to that person.

"After I had already gotten my job in Brazil, the professor took our class for pizza and beer after the last field trip. We were sitting around talking about our plans for Brazil. A woman named Sasha said, 'Wow, I'd love to find a field job like that.' The professor said, 'What's that, Sasha? You need a field job?' And he called over Sandra, one of the teaching assistants, and said, 'Sandra, do you need a field assistant for Samoa?' So Sasha went with Sandra to Samoa. As easy as that."

Toni didn't tag along to Samoa, though. She's done much of her field research in Southeast Asia instead. "Although not without its frustrations, the fieldwork was undoubtedly the most fun part of my dissertation research," she said. "The semester I took off from college probably deserves most of the credit for my current circumstances and the path of study that I chose."

For more information . . .

www.ran.org—The Rainforest Action Network strives to heighten awareness of the dangers posed to the world's rain forests by a variety of entities. The website offers a slew of links to organizations conducting research in the world's rain forests.

Doug Imbruce
COLUMBIA UNIVERSITY
Spent two years running a dot-com

The joke on Doug Imbruce is that if his mother had ever checked under his mattress when he was a teenager, she probably would have found *PC Magazine*, not *Playboy*. "My parents just wanted me to be a normal kid," Doug said. "But I was always geeking out in my room."

Not that they didn't encourage him. "I would find a computer under the Christmas tree the way most kids would find a bicycle," Doug recalled. "The first one my dad bought me had a 386 processor. He'd sit down with me and fool around with it. I fell in love, playing logic games, trying to save maidens from pirates and solving puzzles. I don't know why certain kids take to computers, but for me it represented the opportunity to control my own world. A little kid maybe can't go outside because of the bullies or go to an R-rated movie, but he can sit around in his room and build his own universe on the computer."

As Doug entered his teenage years, the Internet took off, and he soon realized that his skills could be a source of spending money. "My first job was as a Web developer," he explained. "I picked up the phone and called everybody in the Westport [Connecticut] Yellow Pages [to get new clients]. High school was very sheltered, but I liked having adventures. I viewed each visit to a new client as another adventure. Walking in to talk to some forty-year-old guy with a million-dollar company was more fun than sitting in geometry.

"My first customer was a company called Residual Value Insurance. I didn't understand what they did. There was a guy sitting behind a big mahogany desk with his laptop, and he gave me these brochures. I went home and memorized them and then typed up this proposal because I thought that's what you did when you were operating a business. So I faxed these proposals to him, and I guess no one else had approached him about a website or said the right thing."

At the dawn of the Internet age in the mid-1990s, most small-business owners didn't think they could do much more than put those brochures up on the Web. That gave Doug a chance to learn about newer aspects of the technology before his clients heard about them and asked him to do it for them. Meanwhile, he had little idea of what to charge for his services.

"I called other companies and asked them what they were charging, and then I cut it in half," he said. "I figured I should give customers a discount since I was half the age of the people I had called for those price quotes. Plus, I was in my basement, so I could afford to do things cheaply that adults in real offices couldn't afford to do."

Still, Doug was making about forty dollars per hour, and other businesses began to hear about his skills and seek him out. "I was the first kid [at school] to have a cell phone," he recalled. "It was a small community, and people get labels. I was the computer guy with the cell phone. I enjoyed having a label. It was another way of getting validation. Maybe they were making fun of me, but I enjoyed it. I knew who I was and I was comfortable. The big day for me was when the *Westport News* wrote a story about me, and the librarian posted it up on the wall. Everyone was coming up to me congratulating me, and the cheerleaders finally knew my name."

Word continued to spread, and soon Doug was putting his friends to work and taking on clients in New York City. His grades suffered some, but he did well enough in his classes and on the SAT to get himself into Columbia University. "I had this sense that New York City was the end of the universe," he said. "My friends told me that the bar scene there rivaled biblical Sodom in its decadence."

But with his twenty-first birthday still far in the future and increasing amounts of money flowing in from his business, Doug began to wonder whether it made sense to go to college right away. "I didn't really like high school," he said. "I didn't feel like it was a good outlet for my creativity. It wasn't about what you made of it, but what it made of you. And I thought college would be the same thing. It didn't excite me as much as the Internet did.

"I knew there was something else I could do. I couldn't see myself sitting in a dorm room while the Internet was exploding. Instead of making things happen and changing the way the world operated, I'd be throwing back keg shots. I didn't want to sit in a rocking chair later and regret having sat in a classroom reading Descartes while Jeff Bezos was growing Amazon.com."

Doug had only the vaguest sense of what to do with this ambition other than continue to throw brochures up on the Web for local businesses. It was his brother Greg, who was a young investment banker at the time, who helped him think bigger about how he could best use his talents. "As the public became aware of the opportunities to start Web companies, it would only be a matter of time before the pendulum would swing back and the opportunities would be gone," Doug said. "Greg wanted to do it, but he didn't want to do it alone, and I didn't either."

Greg also helped Doug approach their parents, and the two developed a strategy for getting them to let Doug take time off. They thought their father, who had started a medical products company, would appreciate their own entrepreneurial instincts. "What father wouldn't?" Doug asked. "If the father is a farmer and the son says he wants to plant corn, he's stoked."

But their parents weren't exactly stoked. Doug's response was to strike out at them. "The term *hypocrite* is a catch-all used by teenagers to describe, insult, and otherwise demean those in the position of authority, usually parents," Doug explained. "But when I called my dad a hypocrite during our final confrontation regarding the matter of my college education, I was using the word as Webster intended. Dad, in preventing me from starting my own company, was literally acting as a hypocrite since he had been a small-businessman for years."

Doug and Greg's parents, however, were quick to explain that they were just trying to protect Doug. The only reason they were hesitant to give him their blessing is precisely because they knew how hard it would be. "I think my parents weren't so much disappointed as they were worried that I would never have the opportunity again to recapture the innocence of being an eighteen-year-old," Doug said. "They viewed my youth as an oasis. They didn't want me to sacrifice the opportunity to be a kid just because I wanted to be an adult."

Nevertheless, they agreed to cosign the company's incorporation papers on Doug's behalf, since he hadn't yet turned eighteen and couldn't do it himself. There was one condition, though. "Mom and Dad had a separate set of documents for me," Doug recalled. "Deferral papers." He had to sign an agreement that he would go to college after two years, once the business was up and running. So he signed.

As for the business itself, the big idea was to take the work that Doug had been doing on an ad-hoc basis and somehow automate it with software and make it available on a massive scale. "At that point, if a small business didn't have stationery, they could go to Kinko's and get it made," Doug said. "They were an assembly line for printing. We wanted to be an assembly line for Web development, to develop a tool that would make developing a website take one-tenth of the time it would take a custom site built by a consultant to get up and running."

The business was called Buyroad.com, and the tool was located on the site, usable by any customer who paid a subscription fee to access it. "It was a template-driven website creation tool, with six hundred combinations that you could put together in under twenty minutes," Doug explained. "Any business owners could update their site or change it remotely.

"With my old business, most of the money had come from managing and updating the sites for people. What we came to understand was that all these little retail establishments had a mountain to climb. To be able to operate like Amazon, to bring that down to their own level, they needed secure shopping and the ability to take credit cards, so we created a soup-to-nuts solution for them."

That was the promise that Doug and his brother sold to investors, along with a prototype they had worked up. With Greg's connections in the financial community, they were able to raise about $1 million in the fall of 1998 from a collection of high net-worth individuals anxious to get in on the Internet craze. "We hired people to make the prototype scaleable and to help us get clients," Doug said. "That's what we wanted to achieve within a year."

Eventually hundreds of customers were using Buyroad.com's software. "They were all over the country," Doug recalled. "We'd get these e-mails from people saying they'd sold a rug or cup to someone in Alaska. Merchants were so appreciative. There was this big Internet boulder rolling down the hill, and they had thought that they were going to get run over by it. Instead, they were jumping on top of it."

At its peak, Buyroad.com had fifteen people working there, and Doug felt like he was having just as much fun with them as he might have with his freshman roommates. "Eating pizza with four programmers and watching *The Simpsons* before heading back to work to write code so some fashion boutique in Tucson could process a transaction the next day was more fun than sitting there getting rejected by girls and drinking stale beer," he said. "I'd visit friends at Columbia, and they weren't excited. There'd be techno music playing, and they'd all be kind of nodding their heads. You go to college and think you're going to solve the great mysteries of the world after freshman lit class or step straight into an orgy. But neither of those things happen, and it's decidedly normal."

Just as Buyroad.com was starting to gain momentum, however, the stock market turned, and Internet start ups immediately became suspect. "We had just started getting meetings with top-level venture capitalists," Doug recalled. "We'd done what we said we would do. We got our site built and had paying customers. Then the Nasdaq crashed and suddenly it was no more meetings and no more phone calls. It seemed like there were just five days between being the next big thing that was going to get a $10 million investment and not getting any more phone calls and discovering the Internet was dead.

"The last six months weren't anywhere near as much fun as the first eighteen. Telling your employees that there isn't going to be another round of funding. Having to fire someone. I never realized how hard that would be. We fought until the bitter end. We tried to salvage what we could. But we ended up actually getting evicted from our offices. It was like someone stood there and flushed the toilet and our whole office building and all of the companies that had been in there just emptied out."

So Doug started college two full years after he had deferred admission. "I'm older than my classmates, but not by much," he said. "I can speak in front of an eighty-person lecture, knowing that a payroll doesn't rest upon my performance. When my friends stress about finals, I smile and know we'll have the rest of our lives to be under pressure, so I take one of them to the movies."

He's also lost at least some of his cynicism about traditional schooling. "I don't love college," he said. "Part of me finds it boring or stagnant. But I realize now that stagnant can be good. I think if college wasn't a bit stagnant, it wouldn't be the place that it is, the reprieve that it is. In some ways, college is very selfish. All you have to worry about is yourself. To be honest, I've sort of regressed now. My parents think I've never really been a kid, and now I enjoy it. I never missed what I didn't have until I had it.

"So I appreciate college. The barely livable communal bathrooms, the pompous professors, the deadlines and twenty-page papers. Rather than being bitter, constantly thinking of the opportunity lost by spending four years behind a gated campus, I remind myself of the opportunity gained: four years sequestered in a place where your only responsibility is to yourself. No lawyers, no press, no venture capitalists, no employees.

"Not that I didn't love the negotiations, exposure, and excitement that came with running an Internet company. But after spending two years in a suit, wearing gym shorts now and a three-day-old T-shirt is a welcome alternative.

"In retrospect, all I really wanted was to be able to sit a grandkid on my lap and tell him 'I was there.' And I was."

For more information . . .

Your guess is as good as anyone's, since many supposedly in-the-know people are still trying to figure out how to make many dot-coms profitable (eBay has managed to do it). But dot-coms aren't the only type of startup companies out there. And there are just too many books and other resources about starting your own business that we couldn't list them all here. Visit your local book superstore and peruse the business section. Ron wrote a book you might find inspiring: *Upstart Start-Ups!: How 34 Entreprepreneurs Overcame Youth, Inexperience, and Lack of Money to Create Thriving Businesses* (Broadway Books).

Tracy Johnston

WELLESLEY COLLEGE

Worked on Bill Clinton's first presidential campaign

Tracy Johnston was less than two months into her first semester at Wellesley College when she first heard The Voice.

"I was involved in College Democrats at the time, and we were in the living room watching the New Hampshire Democratic Convention. And there was Paul Tsongas and all the others, and it was looking like a pitiful field," she recalled.

"And then I heard The Voice, that unmistakable voice, and he had taken his coat off because he was all pissed and hot, and he was going on about how awful it is that there are all these people who don't have health care in this country. And I said to myself, 'Who is this guy?'"

When Tracy first laid eyes on that televised image of Bill Clinton in October 1991, he had almost no national name recognition, but thanks to a legion of true believers like Tracy, that soon changed.

"The next weekend I drove up to his campaign office, which had just opened, and I sat there and read about him for hours. Finally I said to Chris, this twenty-two-year-old kid who was running the office at the time, 'I'm completely in.'"

Chris tried to convince Tracy to drop out of school and join the campaign right then and there, but she resisted. She had already taken one year off after graduating from the Hackley School in Rye, New York, and she didn't want to pack up and leave again. Yet.

"When I told Chris that I wasn't quite ready to drop out of Wellesley in the middle of my first semester, he didn't push me, but he said that before

I made up my mind for sure, I had to at least hear Clinton speak.

"So when he spoke at the University of New Hampshire, I brought about ten people up. He just glided into the room, and everyone was silent. I was floored. He was the first politician I had ever heard who seemed personally to understand the value of a good education. He talked about lots of things that I really believed in, and then he started talking about the national service program. Our eyes locked for a moment. I started to cry, and instantly there was a connection.

"After that, I had a very hard time concentrating on college. This campaign seemed like the most important thing in the world to me then. I called up my parents and I said, 'You're not going to believe this, but I just met this guy who is going to be president.' They just started getting gray hairs again. I don't do things the easy way.

"I started going up to New Hampshire every weekend. I was so drawn to that life, and I felt that I needed to see what it was like without school hanging over my head."

On January 3, 1992, Tracy moved to New Hampshire to spend her winter vacation working full-time for the campaign. "I lived in Manchester, New Hampshire, in the Clinton hotel. It used to be a hotel or a dorm or something, and there were fifteen of us there during the week. But during the weekends it would swell to three hundred, even though the house only held fifty. So people were all over the floors and the beds.

"We would get up at six or seven every morning and spread out to these little towns all over the state to knock on doors and distribute literature. Then at eleven at night we would all come back and crowd around the television to watch the news and talk politics.

"My three weeks ended, and they asked me to organize Hillary's speech at Wellesley [Hillary Clinton is a Wellesley alumna]. Some of my friends from New Hampshire had already made the decision to leave school. I was toying with the idea, but I wanted to be really sure, so I came back and signed up for classes.

"My first day of classes, I was in physics, listening halfheartedly and writing notes about what I needed to do for the Hillary event. The semester before, I had been so excited about my classes, even when I was working on the campaign, and I realized that something really bad was going on.

"I called my parents right after class, and I told them that I had just sat through a class and not absorbed a word of what the professor was saying. My mother listened to everything, and then she said, and I'll never forget this, 'I don't ever want you to be somewhere and wishing you were somewhere else.'

"My parents came up for Hillary's speech, and it was an absolutely huge success—the best speech I had ever heard anyone give. The place was packed, and it was on the front page of every newspaper. She spoke about her generation, how they lived through the seventies and the greed of the eighties, and how it was their turn now. Their turn to take responsibility for the country and to fix things.

"When we were in private afterward, she started to cry, and she said, 'Thank you, thank you for this day. I really needed to be here today and be reminded that some people still believe in what we are trying to do.' And she looked at me, and I told her that I had decided to leave school to come help them do this, and she said, 'You know, we're trying to fix education here. Bill will be unhappy.'"

But Hillary didn't forbid her to join the campaign, and the next day Tracy and her parents negotiated a tuition refund from Wellesley.

Tracy then returned to New Hampshire. "I worked in the field office all the way through to the end of the primary. We were doing basic grassroots stuff. We were getting people out to hold signs, organizing walking routes for the weekend volunteers, sending out videos of Clinton. People used to be able to name voters in Concord, and I could tell them what street they lived on, what ward they were in, and who they were leaning toward. We were seriously after every single vote.

"The night of the primary was incredible. If we had had another two days, he would have won. That night, he gathered all of us and told us, 'No matter where you go from here, if you go home or if you come to Maine with us, you should never forget what we came here to do.' It got real quiet, and then everyone started to chant, 'We won't forget, we won't forget,' and he leaned forward, came off the platform, and hugged everyone there."

To recover from all the last-minute New Hampshire campaigning, Tracy slept for two straight days. She then hit the road to manage field offices in Maine, Maryland, Michigan, and New York. The other Democratic candidates dropped out one by one, until only Jerry Brown [the former governor of California] was left. Tracy said that she was sure from day one that Clinton would surmount the odds that were stacked against him, but she did have one fleeting moment of doubt in New York.

"There was a paid Brown staffer in the audience one night trying to get Clinton to say that Bush was a racist for vetoing the Civil Rights Act. When Clinton refused, the staffer tore up a Clinton campaign sign in front of all the television cameras there. So the speech had been great, the crowd was enormous, and there was their shot for the news: the tearing-up of our sign.

"I was standing there afterward with another person from the campaign, and we were both crying. How could we get the message out if we couldn't even keep Jerry Brown from orchestrating something like this?

"That moment of doubt lasted about five seconds, because Clinton saw us standing there, and he put a hand on each of our shoulders. We looked up at him, these two teary-eyed kids, and he said, 'It's going to be all right,' and I'm telling you, he was in great spirits, because he knew that it really was going to be alright. That was my one lapse."

After Clinton amassed enough delegates to clinch the nomination, Tracy wasn't sure what to do next. "Toward the middle of April, I called Chris, who by then was handling all the money for scheduling and advance workers at campaign headquarters in Little Rock, and he needed an assistant. [The advance people are in charge of doing everything possible to make the candidates look good on television and ensure that their public appearances go smoothly.] They flew me down, and a few days after I got there, he was promoted, and I took over his job," she said.

"So I was the money chick, just this kid running around to all these departments, trying to make sure there was enough money to cover the expenses of all the people out on the campaign who were doing advance work. Between me and the deputy director of advance, we were responsible for a staff of 120," she said. "I learned a lot about interoffice politics. We were in the tiniest office at first. We had this T-shaped table with all these people crammed around it. I had this little corner, with my calculator and my phone and all these binders, and I had to climb over the table half the time to get out."

The campaign paid her $1,000 a month, which she said was enough to live in a shared apartment in Little Rock. There was just enough left over for some good Southern barbecue and nightly forays to local bars for a little tension release.

"We would work from 7 A.M. till 11 P.M. every day and be so wired by the end that we couldn't go to sleep. So we would go out for food and beer, dance for a couple of hours, and then go back to our apartment to sleep before we started all over again the next day," Tracy said.

After two months of number crunching, Tracy had an epiphany. "It was July almost, and once again I had to decide whether or not I would be going to college the next semester. One day I was sitting at my orange Sears desk, with one phone on my shoulder and one at my ear, and I had my calculator going and all these receipts, and all of a sudden I realized that I was an accountant.

"So I said to Stephen, the guy next to me, 'I'm an accountant. What am I doing with a desk job? I like science, not working at a desk.' So I went outside and took a walk, and when I came back, he asked me if I was all right. 'Yes,' I said, 'but only for Bill Clinton would I do this shit.'"

"It was so exciting to be a part of it, but what I eventually realized was that he didn't need me to get elected. In New Hampshire, it felt as if he needed every one of us giving everything we could to get him elected, but I no longer felt needed. This was not a local thing anymore; this was serious. It couldn't be as informal as it was in New Hampshire. Otherwise, he would have lost. But it was no longer as much fun."

After making the decision to return to school, Tracy went to the Democratic National Convention. "We flew in to New York and landed at about eleven o'clock at night. I was carrying a suitcase with about $200,000 in campaign checks, $50,000 in paychecks, and $30,000 in traveler's checks, all to be delivered to advance staff and various campaign people. It was really heavy."

Tracy enjoyed every minute of the convention. "It was the biggest party I had ever been to, that is, until election night, and then until the inauguration," she said.

Though Tracy made two long weekends out of her trip to Little Rock for the election celebration and to Washington, D.C., for the inauguration, the convention was her last campaign hurrah, and she returned to Wellesley in September.

She threw herself into school with the same fervor that marked her stay in Little Rock. "I became this pumping student. I was taking five classes and three labs, and I set out to get a 4.0 and I did it. I became incredibly focused and efficient, and I completely credit that to my having taken time off," she said.

"I always felt that when I was in college I wanted to be learning a lot in school, so that's what I did. My friends from the campaign would call and didn't understand the names of the classes I was taking. They are still amazed that I made it back here."

Thanks to her efforts in school, but thanks also to her amazing experience outside the classroom, Tracy was awarded a Rhodes Scholarship, just as Bill Clinton was almost thirty years before her. Tracy spent three years at Oxford University in England, first as a student of natural science and later as a social science student. She wrote a thesis on how college students choose majors, then returned to the United States with her soon-to-be husband.

At that point, every conceivable door was open to her: MIT wanted her to enroll and become a rocket scientist, and any number of top corporations and consulting firms would have been glad to have her. Instead she moved to Washington, D.C., and worked for a nonprofit. Eventually, she decided she wanted to be a teacher.

"I do think my experiences will affect me as a teacher," she said. "Half of all people don't vote, but my students won't be among them. Our government is structured in a beautiful way, but most people are cynical about it."

Still, Tracy understands why, for she too has had her faith tested. "I was a true believer," she said. "We had this deep faith in Bill Clinton. But he pounded on the podium and said he did not have sexual relations with Monica Lewinsky. When he lied, it was betraying all of us. I've reconciled with the fact that I was proud of what we were trying to do, even though he didn't turn out to be quite the messenger we thought he was. There was a period of time where I felt that if I had seen him, I would have smacked him."

Nevertheless, Tracy experienced things on the campaign trail that she'll draw on for her whole career as a teacher, or whatever else she chooses to do. "I think I would totally regret not having left school to work on the campaign," she said. "Going straight through school and staying in one city and plowing through and getting married would have left me in a place where I would have woken up one day and realized it was too late. I'm not feeling a burning need now to travel and have adventures, but I'm sure I would feel it if I hadn't done it already."

For more information . . .

www.politicalindex.com—"National Political Index: Contacting National Political Parties." Provides links to all home pages of all political parties in the United States.

www.rnc.org—Official home page of the Republican National Committee: "Welcome to the GOP!"

www.democrats.org—Official home page of the Democratic National Committee.

www.politixgroup.com—Provides links to internship opportunities in politics and government at the White House, think tanks, U.S. Congress, and more.

www.ypa.org—Official website of "Young Politicians of America" offering links to internship centers and programs, including those in the Democratic and Republican parties.

The Road to Victory: The Complete Guide to Winning Political Campaigns—Local, State, and Federal, by Ron Fauchex. Kendall Hunt Publishing Company, 1998. A how-to book with easy-to-read chapters. Warning: This book will be useful but cannot ensure certain victory.

Giev Kashkooli

BROWN UNIVERSITY
Worked for a legal defense service in Harlem and
traveled to Guatemala

During his sophomore year at Brown University, Giev Kashkooli started to question the connections between what he was studying in the classroom and what he was learning outside it.

He was volunteering with abused and homeless children in Providence, Rhode Island, and one boy in particular made him think. "I had a kid ask me once, 'What are you doing here? Are you being paid a lot of money?' I laughed and said, 'I'm here because people like you are teaching me stuff.'"

But when Giev asked himself what he was doing at Brown, he didn't know the answer. "I realized I had no idea what my liberal arts education was preparing me for. I didn't even know if it was useful. I wanted to do something that would help me decide what else I needed to learn while I was at Brown."

Giev started to formulate a plan for his time off that would provide him with an opportunity to learn Spanish, the first language of many of the children he had been working with. "I knew I wanted to live in a city. And I knew I wanted a job that would make me self-sufficient financially. I also hoped the job would let me save enough money to fund the second half of the year, when I wanted to travel and learn Spanish."

Giev had to change his plans slightly when he looked into the cost of living in a major city and learned the salaries offered by most public-service organizations. So he returned home to California for the summer to work with his brother. "We decided to go to all these real-estate agents throughout the Bay Area. When you're trying to sell a house, the agent is always trying to get the owners to fix it up. And the owner never wants to fix it up and mow the lawn, because it costs too much money. Sometimes the agents would pay us themselves. I earned ten dollars an hour for being a handyman—mostly just general gardening and painting. We made up flyers and did the whole thing ourselves. I made a ton of money that summer."

Meanwhile, Giev's search for a job for the fall was proceeding in a somewhat erratic fashion. "By May, I had three job interviews set up. I was thinking, 'This is great; I have this thing taken care of. And then I'll go to Central America.' Then all of a sudden they all fell through. When I went to interview for a job in Boston, they said, 'Actually, we don't have a job available.' I was shocked."

Giev turned to other strategies. "Tell everyone you can that you're planning on taking time off. Tell them what you're doing, because you find things in random places.

"A friend told me he had been at Stanford University's career counseling office and seen a couple of jobs that might interest me. I found a job listing to work with the Neighborhood Defender Service of Harlem as a college intern for about $250 per week. I thought I had hit the lottery. Then I kept reading and came upon the application deadline: July 12. And it was July 13.

"That's another big suggestion. If you really want something, go for it. I called them up and said, 'Look, I really want this job, and I'm perfect for it.' They agreed to send me an application and said they had not yet completed their hiring process."

Giev sent in his application and called NDS each week after that, but they took their time making a decision. "Labor Day weekend rolls around, and I decide to go camping for a few days. So I drive over to Catherine's—my girlfriend's—house and she's shouting at me, 'Giev, your mother's on the phone. NDS just called.'

"They said they still hadn't decided yet. The next thing I remember was, I called them from wherever we were camping. They said, 'Yes, you're hired, but you have to be here on Tuesday.'"

A few days later, Giev flew to New York City and began looking for an apartment.

"I found an apartment within a week. College campuses are really good resources. That's how I found my job, and that's how I came up with a place to live. I arrived in September when all the students were looking for housing and roommates. There were flyers everywhere.

"On Tuesday, I started work at NDS, which is in the heart of Harlem. The next weekend, I looked at ten apartments. One guy wanted to rent me his walk-in closet for $400 a month. Finally I bargained a guy down from $550 to $500 a month. It was near work, so my rationalization was that I would save $60 a month, because I would be the only person in New York who actually walked to work."

Giev finally found out why NDS had been so reluctant to give him a definite answer. "Basically, they told me if I hadn't kept on calling there's no way they would have hired me. They wanted to hire someone from New York. They wanted interns from Harlem and the South Bronx, since those are the communities they serve."

NDS combines social and legal services in one community-based public defender's program. They try to find nonprison sentencing alternatives for people who normally wouldn't be able to afford a lawyer. "My job was to find out what the alternatives were and to present them to the attorney handling the case. I learned how to read a rap sheet, [read] a person's criminal record, investigate a crime scene, and read a police report.

"If you don't have bail money in New York City, you can sit in jail for months before anything really happens. Things get backed up in a big city. Our goal was to be known in the community. That way, if someone got arrested, we could be at the police precinct that night. The person who gets arrested calls Grandma, Grandma calls us, and we go with Grandma.

"First I would try to get as much information as possible from the person who was accused of the crime. Then I would try to get as much information as possible from the victims of the crime. I would tell them who I was and they'd say, 'Wait a minute, you're representing the motherfucker who . . . ?!' I'd say, 'Well, we're representing the person who is *accused* of that.'"

One of Giev's most challenging assignments was to mentor an eighteen year old as part of an alternative sentencing deal. "An NDS attorney I was working with came to me and said, 'Look, Giev, there's this eighteen year old, and I want you to be like his big brother. I want you doing everything with this guy, to keep him out of trouble.'

"I knew right away that was not the best idea. He was one of eighteen children and had a huge rap sheet, mostly for stealing subway tokens to support his crack habit. The last thing a kid with seventeen brothers and sisters needs is another brother.

"So I met with him and asked him, 'What's the deal? What's going on here?' I wanted to know why he had agreed to work with me. His motivation was that he didn't want to be in prison, which I had no problem with. I wouldn't want to be in prison either. The judge told him, 'Okay, I won't put you in prison now, but if you come back here, you're in for two years, not one.' So he took a big-time gamble.

"We were supposed to get him back in school, into a job-training program, and into drug treatment. Turns out he had dropped out of school in seventh grade and hadn't learned anything before or since. He was just worried about getting something to eat. He had been homeless twice. I went to hang out at his place; it was a three-bedroom apartment for fifteen people. There was no electricity. They were heating the place with the oven on full blast. He was definitely taking me places I'd never been before.

"He knew that I couldn't understand his world, and I never pretended to. The kind of stress that this kid was under, facing two years of prison and a drug habit that was kicking his butt, facing the fact that two of his brothers had been killed and that he had no idea who his father was. If he looked at what his life possibilities were, where he was and how far he would have to go . . . . We pulled some strings here and there, I worked my ass off, but he ended up going to prison in the end."

Following a budget was crucial for Giev to make ends meet in New York. "I made sure I brought my lunch to work every day. I spent $35 a week on food. I also planned for my phone bill each month. And I did a lot of walking around the city during my free time."

Giev's job at NDS ended in January and he left for Guatemala a few weeks later. "NDS had many Spanish-speaking clients, so they had a Spanish teacher come in once a week, which helped me get ready for Central America.

"I went to a language school in Guatemala that also taught you about the politics of the country, but I had made a conscious decision not to actually get involved politically. I was going there to learn Spanish. My political activism could come when I was back in the States."

Giev suggests researching Spanish-language schools well ahead of any trip to Central America. "You should make a reservation unless you're willing to be down there not learning Spanish while you wait to get into a class. The first two weeks were exciting but exhausting. I was dreaming verb conjugations. It was an amazing personal experience to communicate with an incredibly limited vocabulary. All I could say was things like 'Hi, my name is Giev. I eat chicken. I like lunch. I brushed my teeth this morning.' If that's all you know, that's all you can talk about," he said.

After three months in Guatemala, Giev traveled to Costa Rica in search of a job that would provide him with room and board in exchange for work. "I found out that it's good to travel with at least two letters of recommendation. When I was applying for jobs in Costa Rica, they wanted letters from institutions in the United States saying, 'In all the time I've known Giev, he has been responsible.'"

Other good information came from fellow travelers, one of whom told Giev about a job opening. "I landed a beauty of a job working in a national park. It was on the coast and extended back into a rain forest. My duties included greeting tourists, digging holes for toilets, cleaning up the beach, and doing trail maintenance. It was unbelievable.

"For the last few weeks, I was stationed by myself. My only job was to make sure nobody was trespassing in the area. There I am, sitting by the ocean, with my whole year behind me. It gave me a great chance to reflect on my time off and think about what I wanted to do when I came back."

Giev came home to Palo Alto, California, and worked as a painter and carpenter to save up money for school. The summer before he graduated, Giev worked with the United Farm Workers (UFW) in California. He then wrote his senior thesis about the organization's history and the impact of agricultural legislation on migrant farm workers. After school, he went to work for UFW and has been with them ever since. "I learned from my experience taking time off that a lot of the inequities I saw in the world had a political and economic basis," he said. "I decided I wanted to learn how to organize for social change, and not do social service work."

More recently, after experiencing the first signs of burnout, Giev took time off again, a two-month unpaid leave of absence from UFW. "I knew it was going to be the right thing and extremely valuable in large part because of the experience of taking the time off from school," he said. "I am back at the UFW, energized, confident that I am in the right place, and feeling liberated because I know I could be doing other things but have chosen to do this work."

For more information . . .

www.ndsny.org—Official website of the Neighborhood Defender Service of Harlem, which offers legal representation to inner-city residents in upper Manhattan.

www.nlada.org—Official website of National Legal Aid & Defender Association, a national organization providing legal representation to low-income clients and their communities. The site offers valuable reference links to local Legal Aid organizations, job and internship opportunities, and general information on the organization.

www.bbbsa.org—Official website of Big Brothers/Big Sisters of America, an organization that provides youth mentoring between adult volunteers and children from primarily single-parent families.

Masa Kenney
UNIVERSITY OF GEORGIA
Fought in the Gulf War

During his teenage years, Masa Kenney cultivated his love for the thrill of the chase. "When we were growing up, we'd go out on camping trips and play paintball and war games and things like that. I don't know if it got into my blood or what, but it was pretty fun," he said.

Masa's middle brother decided to take the war games to another level when he joined the U.S. Army right out of high school. "When I saw what he was getting—about $23,000 to apply to his college tuition for three years in the service—I thought that was a good deal.

"I've always been really independent. I didn't want my tuition to be a burden to my parents. My oldest brother ended up transferring to Emory, and that's one of the most expensive colleges in the country. My dad was having a hard time, always loaning him money. I could see myself getting into a bad situation with it, so I just decided to pay my own way through," he explained.

Masa followed in his middle brother's footsteps and opted for a two-year enlistment in the army. "That's basically the lowest amount of time you can get. I just wanted to go in, get the experience, and get out. For two years, I got about $18,000 to put toward college," he said. (The amount of money you can receive to put toward college costs depends on the length of your service, your age, and the branch of the armed forces you join. It can add up to $25,000 or more for three years of service.)

Though he was recruited in Georgia, Masa was pleased to discover that his destination was at least partly up to him. "It kind of surprised me how everything went. I wanted to travel the world, so I asked for a posting in Europe, and I was able to do it," he said.

Not before he completed eight weeks of basic training under a drill sergeant's watchful eye, however. "You know all those movies you see? Well, I'd seen them too. Basically, everything is true, but unless you've actually been through it, I don't think you could understand," he explained.

"He started cussing at us right away, just giving us the full-force shock treatment. You get that adrenaline rush for the first time, and everything moves really fast. You don't know what's going on. It takes a while to adjust to that level."

Masa did his basic training in Georgia. "The first thing we did once we got there was get in shape. You're going from 5 A.M. to 11 A.M.—calisthenics, marching seven miles with a fifty-pound pack. . . . It's a shock to the system. I'd never fallen asleep standing up before," he said.

The level of pain and suffering that the "cherries," as new recruits are referred to around the army base, must endure is largely up to each unit's drill sergeant.

"They have a basic outline of the program, but they can do little things too. If they catch you without your weapon, they can smoke you and make you do sit-ups and push-ups until you drop. Our drill sergeant made us eat with a spoon. I've eaten salads with just a big spoon. The other thing is, you always had to be done eating before he was. I've eaten entire meals in about a minute."

In the eight weeks of basic training and the optional six-week infantry training that followed, Masa learned the basics of weaponry and some specialized military strategy. "You learn how to throw a grenade, lay out land mines, defuse a mine, receive artillery, read a compass, use a topographical map, and navigate at night. There's a lot that goes into it to get your mind into a total state of awareness and caution."

Naturally, Masa wondered whether he would ever experience combat. "I was actually kind of hoping that I would. You get into a state of mind as to why you're going through this. It's not brainwashing, but it is hammered into your head over and over: It's either kill or be killed. Kill the enemy before he kills you. One shot, one kill," he said.

After his training, Masa was shipped off to a base in Mainz, a town on the Rhine River in southern Germany, where he would be stationed for the next year. "If you're not in the war, you're training for it. That's all you do when you're in the army. We trained for different situations, different terrain. I rode in a tank and trained in these armored boxlike vehicles that they used in Vietnam. We called them aluminum coffins," he said.

Once a soldier finishes basic training, the army becomes more like a nine-to-five job. Masa took advantage of the milder routine to soak up some European culture. "I traveled to Paris and Bavaria. I got to go to a ballet, and I saw some of Chagall's work. I got to experience a lot of things I'd never have the chance to do in the States," he said.

He was also able to strike up a friendship with some Germans, especially those who shared his fondness for sampling the local brews in pubs near the base. "I fell in love with that beer. They really know how to party over there, and I quickly found out how alike we all are, no matter what culture we're from.

"Some things are very different, too. The Germans really look down on violence. A lot of the younger people did not like American soldiers at all. But with the older people, you still get the feeling that you're welcome there and that they remember what we did to help them rebuild after World War II."

After one year in Germany, Masa was preparing to return to the States to finish his tour of duty. Everything changed, however, when Saddam

Hussein's forces invaded Kuwait and George Bush ordered them out by January 15, 1991. "Basically, as soon as they changed my plans and told me I would be staying on in a different unit, I knew I would be going to the Middle East if there was a war. It was hard, though, because it was difficult to get information. Once a base was put on alert that they would be going to the Middle East, they couldn't make any outgoing calls. There's a real tight lid on security," he said.

"Lots of things were going through my mind while we were waiting to be put on alert. My family. My country. I knew I might die."

Masa said that he wasn't aware of the controversy that was raging at home over the war. "In the army newspaper, they made Saddam out to be Hitler. If I had known about some of the political aspects and the oil money, I might have been more against it. But I didn't understand any of that.

"All they told us was that this big country had invaded this little country and that our job was to go in and kick the big country's ass. I didn't have any doubts. Basically I was being sent in to do what I was trained to do, and that's what I wanted to do. I was in a state of mind where I was going to go in and shoot a little girl if I had to, if I thought she was carrying a hand grenade behind her back," he said.

Masa's unit was the last one to land in Saudi Arabia before the air war began. "When the Scuds first started flying around, we had been sitting, about 500 of us, in this huge warehouse. Outside, all of a sudden, we saw this yellow streak flying across the sky. When we went out to look, we saw a red streak flying in from the other direction to meet it: a Patriot missile.

"Everyone had to get back in to throw on MOPP gear [protective clothing] in case they were using chemical weapons. When the Patriot took it out, there was a huge boom, and all this screaming. The explosion was so huge that these enormous ships in port started banging against one another because of the waves that the boom caused. It was the first big shock I had while I was over there," he said.

When the ground war began, there were other surprises. Masa had hoped to fight with his entire military unit intact. Instead, he was assigned to the dieseling unit. "That was the lifeline out there. Nobody could go anywhere without diesel, so I ended up riding this huge fuel tank. It was basically a time bomb [if it got hit].

"We advanced with the front lines, so we could see everything that was going on. We moved forward deep into Iraq to cut off their retreating lines. That's when I started seeing all the action: the wreckage, the fires, the bodies everywhere. We basically pulverized them," he said.

After the war, Masa's division got assigned to cleanup duty. "We were the last group in, so we had to stay. They had evacuated all these civilians because of the oil fires, and I ended up being stationed there for six weeks. The conditions were so bad that it would be dark in the middle of the day, and when it rained, you could see the soot on your arms."

After several more months in Germany, Masa returned to the United States and graduated from the University of Georgia in 1996 with a degree in landscape design. Like many veterans of the war against Iraq, Masa has experienced several symptoms of Gulf War Syndrome. "The fires, maybe in combination with some of the inoculations they gave us; that's supposedly what caused it. It's everything from nervous twitches to diarrhea and nausea. The problem is, the symptoms are not specific enough to really pinpoint any source. I've had a lot of trouble since then. I've made at least six trips to the Veterans Administration Hospital, but they're basically saying that I'm all right. I know my body, and I know if something is wrong with it or if it's changed. The government still hasn't taken responsibility for what's occurring. They sent hundreds of thousands of people over there, and I think their biggest fear is having to pay out money to all these people."

Masa's health has slowly improved since the war, and he's had enough energy to start a landscaping business in Athens, Georgia, where he went to school. "Designing and planting plants is therapeutic and it calms me," he said. Though he had been worried about how the fires and fallout would affect his ability to have children, he's now the father of a six-year-old boy.

Though Masa's army days are over, he still thinks of his tour of duty often, especially now that Iraq is on the global radar screen once again. "It grates on my nerves to see us talking about going back," he said. "We could and should have done it right the first time."

For more information . . .

See General Resources, Work in the United States, Military, page 234.

Kristin Levine
SWARTHMORE COLLEGE
Worked as an au pair in Austria

Kristin Levine's journey from Virginia to Vienna began when she was leafing through titles in a used-book store during her senior year of high school. "I like to go to bookstores and look at old books. I happened to come across one about finding jobs overseas in Europe, and I bought it on a whim," she recalled.

At the time, Kristin had been accepted at Swarthmore College and received permission to defer her matriculation for one year. "My whole life, people like my mother always promised me, 'Oh, when you get to junior high, you'll like school better.' And then, 'Oh, when you get to high school, you'll like that better.' And I never did. I didn't believe anyone who told me that when I got to college it would be different and that everything would be better."

Kristin's used book included the address of an au pair agency in Vienna, and she wrote to ask for the necessary application forms.

Paperwork was not her only obstacle, however. "When I told one of my teachers, he said, 'Just don't get married and have kids. That happened to a niece of mine.' He thought I was going to Austria to get married to a rich baron or something. My English teacher said the same thing. It was ridiculous."

Additional resistance came from people in her community who were mystified by the idea of taking time off. "Many of the people in my town are lawyers and government people. They are very into getting ahead on the fast track. To them, taking a year off means you lose a potential year of making money. And why on earth would anyone want to do that? Thankfully, my parents were very supportive of my idea."

The au pair agency Kristin wrote to placed her with a family in Vienna. Upon arrival, she was given a brief orientation by the agency, and both she and her employers were required to sign a contract.

"The contract stated all the rules," she explained. "You are supposed to work five hours a day, six days a week. You must be given one day a week totally off. You must also be given your own private room and have your board provided for. The family is required to give you time to attend language classes if you want to. Finally, the family is to give you a weekly stipend, which for me amounted to roughly seventy dollars per week. It's a great deal. Anyone can do what I did as an au pair. All they have to do is come up with the money for the plane ride over, which is not paid for."

Kristin was also expected to help with household chores. "One day I was working in the bathroom and I thought, 'I bet no one expected that Kristin the National Merit Scholar would end up scrubbing toilets in Austria.' That's so great. I don't want to scrub toilets forever, but it wasn't bad for a year. You learn how to do it."

Kristin also learned to live on her own for the first time. "Many au pairs live in the house with the family they work for, but I did not," she said. "I lived about a twenty-minute walk away in a room that belonged to a friend of theirs. I had a room, a toilet, and a sink in my room. And that was it, no fridge, no stove, nothing.

"The advantage was that when I was off at the end of the day, I was really off," she recalled. "No one could say, 'Oh, could you watch the kids while I'm making dinner?' I had to go through two huge doors and up a flight of winding stairs to get to my rustic little room. I ended up loving it. I always felt like I was a starving artist living in a bohemian garret."

Kristin had the good fortune to be matched with a wonderful family. "I cannot say enough nice things about them," she said. "The mother, Eva, was a TV reporter for the Austrian Broadcasting System. She would always rush home because she wanted to watch herself on the news. The father, Stefan, worked for the Green Party and knew lots of important people. The mayor of Vienna came over one afternoon for lunch.

"I hoped to really be treated like a member of the family, and I actually was. I became friends with the family's friends, met their relatives, went on vacation with them, was invited whenever they gave a party, and was generally treated with great kindness and respect."

Kristin's main responsibility was to pick up Phillipe from kindergarten every day at two-thirty in the afternoon and stay with him until his parents got home, which would be between five and seven. "When it was warm enough, we would go to the park. We spent a lot of time reading, playing games, and building with blocks," Kristin said.

"Phillipe and I had a schedule going, with lots of activities. On Mondays, I picked him up and brought him to a friend's house. There would be five or six little kids, and the music teacher would come. They all sat there and sang songs. I would sit with all the mothers and drink tea and argue about which was the best method to teach kids music. It was great for me to spend time with adults, mainly mothers in their thirties. I feel that I really learned a lot from them, and they treated me like an adult."

Kristin underestimated how hard it would be to take care of children. "Suddenly you're a mommy for five hours a day. It's very different from baby-sitting. You're not only responsible for making sure the kid doesn't get hurt. You have to learn how to discipline kids and teach them things. If you're depressed when the kid comes home from school, you're going to have to entertain him and make sure that he's okay. And if he misses his mother, you're going to have to comfort him, even if you miss yours."

The family Kristen worked for was very happy to have her, because their last three or four au pairs hadn't worked out very well. "They were interested in going to discos every night until 4 A.M. and drinking," she explained. "You can't party until 4 A.M. every night and be a good au pair in the morning."

In her spare time Kristin pursued her goal of becoming fluent in German and learning more about opera. Being required to speak English with Phillipe made learning German more difficult. To learn faster, Kristin took German classes on Tuesday and Thursday mornings at the university.

"Classes were great," she recalled. "Most of the other students were also au pairs. Many were from former Communist countries; a lot were from the Netherlands. We had the most fascinating discussions. A woman from Russia would express her viewpoint, a woman from the Czech Republic would disagree, a woman from Norway would continue, and I would be called upon to express the American viewpoint."

During her year in Vienna, Kristin saw more than twenty operas. "This started as a minor interest and quickly became a passion," she said. "Standing room at the Vienna State Opera costs $1.50. The first time, it was hard figuring out which line to stand in and where to go, but I soon became a pro."

Kristin loved waiting in line. "People wore everything from blue jeans to tuxedos. There were always a few people reading the libretto or studying the score and conducting the opera silently to themselves. I met the most interesting people: a man from Japan who was in Vienna for a human rights conference; an older Austrian man, dressed in a dapper gray suit, who lamented the new set for Wagner's *Ring*; an American woman on vacation; and a guy studying to be a doctor in Australia."

Kristin also took an opera class with friends who shared her enthusiasm. The group met at different people's houses and would watch a video of the opera they planned to see. They also studied the libretto and learned the basic musical themes. "The best part was when the teacher got opera singers to come and sing for us," she said. "It sounds absolutely incredible to hear an opera singer in someone's living room."

Kristin's advice to people considering working overseas as an au pair is to apply for a transfer if they don't get a good family. "You hear horror stories sometimes. Many au pairs come from former Communist countries in Eastern Europe and are there illegally. Some of the families look on them as cheap labor. People took advantage of some au pairs and had them work twelve-hour days, doing all the washing and ironing and sharing a room with the kids. A lot of bad situations can occur, like fathers that would make passes at the au pairs.

"Everyone should realize that they have a right to change families anytime. You can leave at any moment. If it's a bad situation, don't put up with it. Be assertive when you think people are treating you unfairly," she said.

Kristin suggests checking with the family ahead of time to clarify expectations on both sides. "A prospective au pair should be able to find out what the job will be, the hours she'll be working, and where she'll be living. The more you can find out from the family beforehand about what you're going to be doing, the better off you're going to be," she said. And it is worth noting that men can also apply to be au pairs—traditionally thought of as a young woman's job—though some families do prefer women.

Kristin was originally anxious about making friends. "I thought it would be very hard to make friends, and actually it was not. The adults I met all treated me as an equal, which really meant a lot to me. I knew an opera singer, a math professor, a painter, a biologist, and lots of people from the foreign service. Austrians can be very private, but eventually I became friends with the neighbors and other Austrians my own age.

"In Austria, if I wanted friends, I had to go out and make them. If I was standing in line at the opera and feeling lonely and wanted to talk to someone, I would go up to people who were talking about something interesting and just sort of join in. You might have to give yourself a pep talk, but once you realize you can do it, it starts to build," she said.

"In high school I felt like I had been put in such a pigeonhole. I had a role to fulfill as the good student, the good daughter, never staying out late or breaking the rules. In Austria, I could try new things.

"I also learned to drink. I never drank in high school and I was worried that everyone in college would be pressuring me to drink. Or that everyone would be drinking and that I wouldn't want to. There are no drinking-age laws [in Austria] and they have a more normal way of drinking. Nobody gets drunk at a party; they just enjoy a glass of wine, and nobody makes a big deal of it."

Coming home was hard for Kristin. "I felt there wasn't anyone who was able to understand how much the experience had meant to me. When you come home, everyone expects you to be happy about coming home. You are, but there are still things you miss [about where you were]."

Kristin's attempts to introduce her friends to long afternoon chats over tea and evenings at the opera were met with mixed results. "I brought a tea set home with me. When I invited some friends over for tea, they said, 'Tea? I don't really like tea.' I said, 'Try it; you might like it.' They did and told me it was kind of yucky," she said. She did, however, manage to get an opera club started at Swarthmore.

Though Swarthmore has a reputation as academically grinding, taking time off had been an even greater challenge for Kristin. "Going to Vienna to work as an au pair was by far the hardest thing I have ever done. I was homesick for the first three months. All of a sudden I was in a country where I knew absolutely no one and didn't speak the language very well.

Sometimes I felt extremely lonely and tired of always having to make such an effort to say and do the simplest things. There were days when I woke up and felt like crying," she said.

"But throughout it all, no matter how depressed I was at times, whenever I asked myself the questions 'Is this worth it? Is this really what I want to be doing?' the answer was always 'yes.'"

Flowing from her experience in Germany, Kristin eventually decided to major in German. And her experiences with Phillipe had given her the teaching bug, so she got certified and taught third grade after graduating from Swarthmore. Over the years, however, she'd also picked up a keen interest in film. Having taken one big risk already by working in Austria, she decided to take another by chasing her dream of screenwriting before she had kids and additional responsibilities of her own.

After earning an MFA in film and electronic media, she starting teaching screenwriting and found she enjoyed working with older students. So in addition to teaching writing, she's also been teaching German part-time in a local high school. All along, she's been trying to sell her screenplays and has been a finalist in several screenwriting contests. Next up: an effort to write and direct her own short film with a friend.

"Going to Vienna obviously has had an impact on my career, since I am still teaching German part-time, but it had an even bigger impact on my attitude toward taking risks," Kristin said. "Whenever I'm scared about trying something new—directing this film comes to mind—I think back to the fact that I went to live in a foreign country when I was eighteen. Since I was able to handle that, surely this situation will turn out okay too."

For more information . . .

www.interexchange.org—Click on "Working Abroad" to learn about au pair programs in France, Germany, Holland, and Spain.

www.greataupair.com—Matchmaker website for au pairs and families, national and international.

www.aupairsearch.com—Matchmaker website for au pairs and families, national and international.

Carrie Lee Newman
UNIVERSITY OF WASHINGTON
Worked as a deckhand on a boat in Alaska

Carrie Lee Newman's progression from landlocked bluegrass girl to Alaskan sea dog began when she was in third grade.

Carrie's third-grade teacher brought records of whale songs that came inserted in *National Geographic* magazines into the class and played them. "I was absolutely enchanted. Studying the songs of humpback whales became a passion. I listened to more *National Geographic* records in my high school library than I ate square pizzas in its cafeteria," Carrie said.

Because there are very few whales in Kentucky, Carrie knew that she would have to move someplace else if she wanted to study them. "It just isn't possible to fulfill dreams of life at sea when you are in Kentucky," she explained.

When Carrie finished high school in Louisville, she enrolled in the honors program at Northern Kentucky University. "I went to NKU with the idea that I would get all my general requirements out of the way, save money, and get out of Dodge as quickly as my fins could paddle me," she said.

Carrie decided to major in biology and started looking into transferring. She hoped to move to a coastal school after her second year at NKU. "Two years turned into three, because I didn't have enough money, although heaven knows I was just raking it in as a work-study student," she said with irony.

Two and a half years after Carrie graduated from high school, Arthur Davidson came to NKU to deliver a lecture. He had written the text for

Circle of Life, a book that features photographs of the rites of passage practiced by cultures around the world. Carrie had been so excited by a story about the book she had seen in *LIFE* magazine that she arrived half an hour early for Davidson's lecture.

"I was sitting in the auditorium, and a man came in and struck up a conversation with me. I asked him where he was from and he said, 'Alaska.' I told him I had always dreamed of going to see the humpback whales there. In high school I painted a big humpback whale on my backpack with the word 'ALASKA' in enormous letters below it."

When the man was done talking with Carrie, he got up on stage and began his lecture. She had been talking to Davidson himself, and he was impressed enough by Carrie that he promised to look into finding a way to get her to Alaska. "He called a friend of his who owned a cruise line and asked if they had a job opening for me. At the time, they didn't."

When Carrie moved back home to Louisville the following summer, she had already made up her mind not to go back to NKU. She was even prepared to accept a job that involved water with more chlorine in it than whales. "I had gotten my lifeguard's certification and was tucking my tail between my legs as I imagined a long summer of whistle twirling at the pool," she said.

Shortly after she arrived home, Carrie called up her college roommate to check in. "She gave me the news that the people from the cruise line had called. Someone on their crew had quit, and the job was mine if I wanted it. When could I be in Anchorage, they wanted to know. I called them immediately and accepted the position. I had just enough money in my bank account for a one-way plane ticket to Alaska."

Carrie sprung the news on her unsuspecting parents the next morning at breakfast. "I told them, 'I'm leaving for Alaska. I got a job on a boat in Prince William Sound.'" Carrie's parents thought there should have been plenty to keep her busy right there in Louisville. "They were shocked. They practically stood in the driveway to keep me from leaving. They had a difficult time accepting my desire for self-reliance and independence," she said.

The trip from Louisville to Anchorage was a long one, and Carrie was exhausted when she arrived. From Anchorage she boarded a bus to Whittier, fifty miles east of the city, where she was to meet up with the rest of the crew. "It's gorgeous up there. Pure wilderness. There is simply nothing out there but you and planet Earth."

Carrie worked as a deckhand and stewardess on a tour boat that made daily trips in and around Prince William Sound. When they arrived back in Whittier, Carrie cleaned and restocked the boat. "Days were long— sometimes seventeen hours if we did two full tours. Our passengers came from Anchorage every day. We took them out for a day of wildlife watching. Whales, porpoises, otters, Dall's sheep, black bears, bald eagles . . . you name it," she said.

The boat also traveled amid dozens of glaciers. "The highlight was the active tidewater glaciers. We could get right up next to those and watch them calve. Sometimes an enormous mass of ice would fall off the face of the glaciers into the sea. People would always ask me, 'Don't you get tired of seeing the same thing every day?' I never saw the same thing twice in Alaska," she said.

The job lasted until late September, and the boat headed down to Seattle. "I walked around alone the night we arrived and instantly fell in love with Seattle. It was one of the most striking cities I had ever seen," she said.

The next morning, Carrie boarded the plane home to Louisville. "I had obligations to tie up at home before I could make the move out west. Kentucky was great for about a week, but after that I was just overwhelmed with a feeling of stagnation. I had seen all these things I had waited so long to see. How could I settle for the river when I could have the ocean?"

Carrie got a job at Victoria's Secret and started to pool her earnings with her Alaska money. She had begun to save for what she hoped would be her move to a coastal school. Her parents, on the other hand, wanted her to re-enroll at NKU and get her degree.

"I finally told them one day, very calmly, 'What you don't understand is that I am going to leave. I am not asking for your permission, but I would like your blessing.'" With that, Carrie packed up her car in March 1993 and left Kentucky for good.

"Up in Alaska, someone told me about the program at the University of Washington in Seattle. During my time back in Kentucky, I had researched the school and found the tuition to be reasonable. Plus, I adored Seattle. I would move there, try to get into UW, and work on establishing my residency to get the tuition down," she said.

But not before she went to Alaska for another season. This time, Carrie had gotten a job on a boat that was in a bad state of repair. "I began to assist in the total overhaul of the boat from the water up. It was grueling work, but I actually enjoyed it. I was the only woman in the shipyard. It was quite an experience, going from Victoria's Secret in my stockings and heels to a shipyard in my coveralls, knee pads, and hard hat," she said.

The boat sailed north in May, and Carrie spent her second summer cruising the whale-laden waters of Prince William Sound. At the same time, she applied to the University of Washington for the fall. They rejected her.

Refusing to take no for an answer, Carrie asked two former professors at NKU to write letters of recommendation to the board of admissions. She successfully appealed its decision and was admitted to UW for the winter quarter.

"I was lucky. By the grace of the gods, nearly every single credit from NKU transferred. I had managed to complete all my general requirements as far as UW was concerned and could focus on my degree work," she said.

Carrie's persistence had won her parents over, and they were now supporting her ambitions. Despite their help with tuition costs, however, she still had to work full-time as an office manager to support herself.

"I found I had little in common with other college students who were completely supported by their parents. My job always came first. I had to skip classes for work because they were depending on me for one thing or another," she said.

Carrie plans to pursue a Ph.D. "They change the name of my field by the minute. Cetology, marine biology, psychology/animal behavior, biological oceanography . . . you name it. I want to study the humpback populations in the Southern Hemisphere, because those whales are largely undocumented," she said.

She has also logged enough hours at sea to qualify for a license that allows her to operate some boats under certain conditions. After one more summer she will be eligible for her captain's license, which will give her even more of a passport to the world's oceans. "That's been the goal all along. To break out from under the burden of my own limitations."

For more information . . .

www.coolworks.com—Job site providing many links to various outdoor employment opportunities all over, including Alaska.

www.aquaculture.com—Job site listing aquaculture jobs from research assistant to marine biologist to deckhand.

www.dnr.state.ak.us/parks—Official website of the Alaska Department of Natural Resources, Division of Parks and Outdoor Recreation.

www.jobmonkey.com—Provides links to information about some of the coolest jobs on earth, including outdoor employment opportunities in Alaska, cruise liners, and national parks.

Part 2

Volunteer

Laura Castro
GROSSMONT JUNIOR COLLEGE
Served in the California Conservation Corps

Indoor learning never held much appeal for Laura Castro. Though she was an honors student in junior high, a decided lack of effort and motivation marked her experience at San Diego High School. "I was in all advanced classes, but I was just too lazy to do the work," she recalled. "I would go home and I basically just wouldn't do anything."

Though Laura had a tough time putting her finger on the exact source of her malaise, her verdict on high school couldn't be clearer. "I just didn't like it at all," she said.

When it came time to decide what to do after high school, Laura wondered if going straight to college would be wise. "I realized that I was not going to do very well if I went to college with the same attitude I had in high school."

Laura also knew she would never want to be stuck working in an office from nine to five. "Ever since I can remember, I have wanted to be a wildlife biologist. I have loved animals and being outdoors all my life."

Her opportunities to pursue wildlife biology were limited by the cost of expensive summer enrichment programs that would have allowed her to explore the field. The summer before her senior year, however, she found paying work in a summer conservation corps near her home. Signing on for a full-time stint in the state's conservation corps seemed like a natural way for her to continue to explore a career in the outdoors.

The California Conservation Corps is proud of its unofficial motto: Hard work, low pay, and miserable conditions. "The recruiters don't tell you very much when you sign up," Laura recalled. "They don't want you to know how hard you're going to work."

Almost any college-age California resident is eligible. Most sign on for a year and rotate between several work centers all over the state. The centers serve as base camps for the small groups of young people that fan out to work in the state's parks and forests.

Corps members wear uniforms, get up with the sun, and often work late. For their efforts they earn minimum wage and a small scholarship toward college. The corps is incredibly diverse from a demographic perspective, and most recruits enter with only a high school education or less.

Laura arrived for her two-week training session with high hopes but few expectations. The most immediate surprise, she said, was realizing how different she was from many of the other corps members. "Many of the people there were having problems at home and their parents forced them to join, or they were trying to get away from gangs, or their parole officer forced them to go. I was a little bit shocked."

The two weeks of training were intense. Laura learned to administer first aid, handle power tools, and fight fires—all things that she had never done before and had not expected to be doing. "They worked us hard. Up at dawn, running, then back for breakfast, then training all day long. The leaders were very mean, but we learned a lot."

For her first assignment, she spent seven months at the corps' Porterville Base Camp, near Sequoia National Park. From there, with her crew leader and a team of twelve, she maintained nature trails, cleared streams, and did other upkeep work in the state's national parks.

Though the crew came from a variety of backgrounds, group dynamics were no problem, according to Laura. "The only problem was the attrition rate, which is pretty high. People are coming and going a lot, so you just have to get used to new people coming in."

For Laura, however, being part of the group, especially after hours, was difficult for a variety of reasons. "It mostly had to do with my personality. I was very, very shy. I didn't really talk to anybody outside of work except my roommate for the first four months. I was very antisocial."

Eventually, however, as her crew members got to know her, they came to admire her. "I think the guys respected the fact that I worked really hard. When I finally started talking, I think it made a big difference in terms of their opinion of me."

After her seven-month stint at Porterville, Laura's group leader encouraged her to apply to a backcountry crew. Working backcountry for the CCC is like being a Green Beret in the Marines; it means you're the cream of the crop and you get sent out into the wilds to tackle some of the toughest, most rewarding projects.

"At first I didn't really want to go to backcountry," she recalled. "People talk about it, how intense it is, and it seemed really scary to me. It was not so much living out in the woods as it was living with people I didn't know."

The backcountry lived up to its reputation. "Every day we'd wake up, get outside fast, hike into the woods fast. Everything was fast, fast, fast. They were teaching us how to mark and fix trails, build stone steps, and make walls on the sides of trails."

The crew began moving around to different sites to work on various backcountry trails. Some locations were so remote that their food and supplies had to be brought in by mule. "It was fascinating," Laura recalled. "Each site, we got to do something different. The rock stairs were especially neat, because you were designing your own work. You had to find just the right rock, so it was like a puzzle. It was fun."

As her five-month backcountry assignment wore on, Laura found that the experience was tougher mentally than it was physically. Once again, she said she found herself set apart from the group, though it was not her shyness this time.

"There was this guy there, a Forest Service supervisor actually, who wouldn't accept me because I was Catholic. He would make all these comments and try to get me to read books that painted a negative image of God. It was basically a prejudice. If it had just been him, it would have been fine, but he also got one of my crew members to bother me about it, and that was just too much for me to handle. I had never really had any problems with people before, and I didn't know how to defend myself very well."

As difficult as it was, however, the experience had its upside. "I had to learn to become more aggressive and assertive," Laura said. "I had never talked back to a superior before, but there I finally had to learn to just fight with him."

By the time backcountry ended, Laura's twelve months were up, but she petitioned for a longer stay in the corps and was allowed to continue for another year. She moved on to Elkhorn Slough, a much smaller CCC center near the Pacific Ocean, between Monterey and Santa Cruz.

There, she began an internship with a wildlife biologist. Her responsibilities included watering plants on nature trails, planting vegetation, clearing overgrown brush with a chain saw, constructing signs for the trails, and learning about the local wildlife.

Though the experience was interesting, Laura quickly realized that it was not the kind of wildlife biology she wanted to pursue as a career. "It confused me at first, because I didn't realize that not all wildlife biology is like that. I want to be out in the field, seeing animals in their natural environment. My boss spent a lot of time in his office."

After eight months at Elkhorn, Laura was selected to join a group of corps members and college students who would spend the next two months conducting a comparative ecological study of Lake Baikal in Siberia and Lake Tahoe.

For Laura, who had never left California before except to visit relatives who lived just over the border in Mexico, the experience was mind-blowing. "Lake Baikal was absolutely beautiful," she said. "There are a lot of stereotypes about Siberia being all snowy and desolate, but the area around the lake is wonderful."

The students and CCC crew members studied with a group of Russian students in Siberia and then served as hosts when the group returned to study Lake Tahoe.

Laura finally left the corps a short time after she returned from Lake Tahoe. She started working as a teacher's aide in Santa Cruz and then returned to San Diego the next summer and found a similar job. That fall she also began taking classes at Grossmont Junior College near San Diego, with an eye toward getting her general education credits and a few basic science courses out of the way before transferring to an out-of-state school that had field-study programs for biology majors.

"I'm doing so well in school now, it almost seems easy. Or at least a lot easier than I thought it would be," she said. "It's so hard to explain, but I guess after all that time away just thinking about my academics and my future, I got motivated. I really enjoy school now."

Laura said that the extent to which her two years of hard labor changed her was shocking at first. But, she insists, she would hardly do anything differently if she had it to do over again.

The CCC is open only to California residents, but many states have developed similar programs under the National Service Bill. "Now," Laura said, "I try and convince everyone else to join the Corps, too."

For more information . . .

www.ccc.ca.gov—The California Conservation Corps brings California residents between the ages of eighteen and twenty-three together for a yearlong program of outdoor service projects. Students receive minimum wage, subsidized housing, and a small stipend. (800) 952-5627.

Tim Holtan
UNIVERSITY OF MARYLAND—COLLEGE PARK
Worked at an orphanage in Vietnam

Tim was born in Vietnam two years before the fall of Saigon. He knows that his father was a soldier killed in the war and that his mother left him at an orphanage, hoping that he'd be adopted by someone who could take better care of him.

He was evacuated from the country—he's still not sure how—and brought to the United States soon afterward. His adoptive parents, who at the time believed they were infertile, picked him up at the Baltimore, Maryland, airport when he was two years old and took him home. Eventually they adopted two more children, this time from Korea. Not long afterward, Tim's adoptive mother was able to get pregnant and had two more kids.

The whole Holtan brood spanned just five years in age and grew up together. "We all had very similar experiences, playing sports and Little League baseball, doing gymnastics," Tim said. "I had a good childhood."

While Tim knew he was adopted, he had only the vaguest of notions that he was truly different from the other kids in his town. "It's one of those things that you don't notice until people start pointing it out to you," he said. Today, it's common for parents who have adopted children from certain countries to have playgroups with other parents who have adopted kids from the same place. Still, Tim was one of just a few Asian children in his school. "My mother did belong at the time to Catholic Charities of Baltimore, where they had a support group with families who had adopted kids from all over the world," he recalled. "But I was seven or eight at the time, and I couldn't have cared less about the differences among everyone. I was just trying to be like the other kids."

As Tim navigated his teenage years, however, he began to have a nagging sense that he was missing out on part of who he was. "The most Asian I ever felt was when we would go to a Chinese restaurant, and that wasn't even my heritage," he said. "Even when I occasionally went to a Vietnamese restaurant, I still felt like an outsider because I didn't understand the culture. I grew up as an American, with Caucasians all around me."

While high school offered little opportunity for social mobility, college beckoned as a chance for Tim to test out life on his own. "High school was easy," he said. "You knew exactly what you were going to do and where you had to be and at what time. In college I wanted to see if I could make it on my own. Going away to the West Coast and dealing with things myself—instead of coming home to Mom and Dad every night—would be different."

Tim chose to attend Foothill College in Los Altos, California, and socially the experience was everything he had hoped it would be. "It sounds funny, but there were more Asian women there than I had ever seen in my life," he recalled. "I didn't really date in high school, and now I had the opportunity to do it without Mom and Dad telling me to be home in bed at a certain time. I was out clubbing until four or five in the morning.

"You can probably guess that my grades kind of suffered because of that. I knew I needed to either pull it together or make some other kind of change. While I knew that people were finishing four years of school and going on for master's degrees and doctorates, I was also becoming more of a free thinker. The lifestyle in California was different from what I was used to, not as fast-paced as the East Coast and with different kind of people."

As comfortable as Tim was with his new friends in his new surroundings, he still didn't feel completely at ease in California's Vietnamese community. "They didn't really look at me as being Vietnamese," he said, since he had grown up in the States, didn't speak the language, and knew little about the culture.

Then, out of the blue, he got an opportunity that would change all that. Inspired by her own joy she found in giving homes to kids who had none, Tim's mom had trained as a social worker and gone to work for an adoption agency. When a friend of hers told her that her daughter was working at an agency in Vietnam and needed some help, she told Tim, knowing that he was restless in California and looking for a way to spend some time away from the classroom.

Tim jumped at the chance to return to the country where he was born and help orphans get the same help he had almost twenty years before, even if the details of the job were not clearly outlined. "I knew where I'd be staying and who I'd be working for, but I didn't arrive with any set guidelines for what I'd be doing on the job," Tim recalled. "I did know that I wouldn't be getting paid at first, so I worked waiting tables to make enough money to live that first year." Since living expenses were so much less in Vietnam than they were in California, Tim managed to make ends meet until the agency began paying him a stipend.

Since Tim's foreign language skills were limited, he offered his expertise in another language he'd been developing in classes at Foothill: accounting. He also helped arriving American families make arrangements to take their new children home. "It was called the 'Orderly Departure Program,'" he explained. "In order to get a visa, the kids had to have physicals to show that they had no diseases. Families went to Bangkok in Thailand to do this, so I would escort them there, pick up paperwork, and set up appointments with the embassy." He also served as a de facto tour guide, helping families see the sights in both Bangkok and Vietnam as they waited for a date for their official adoption ceremony to be set.

Occasionally when things were slow at the agency, Tim hired himself out as a tour guide and got paid for it. "Expats usually find each other," he explained, noting how many people from other countries tend to make friends with one another when they're living far from home. "I networked with other foreigners, mostly Australians, who would give my name to people who wanted to tour around."

While Tim networked with other English-speakers to find a way to earn a bit of extra money, he mostly avoided the increasing number of Americans who were flocking to the country to teach English or start businesses. "I was trying hard to live like a local," he explained. "I didn't go over there to eat hamburgers and hot dogs. I was too busy hanging out in local bars, and I was dating Vietnamese women."

Finding love—or at least chasing it—in a foreign country is one sure way to pick up the local language quickly. "You can understand a lot after just a few months," Tim said. "But speaking well took a whole year. I went into the job with the attitude that I would spend at least a year and tough it out, but it was lonely at first. I didn't have any friends, and without knowing the language you can't really communicate with anyone. I spent a lot of time at first watching TV I didn't understand and listening to music I had brought with me.

"That first year was harder than any year I had ever spent in school," Tim recalled. "I tell friends of mine about it now, and they think it sounds so glamorous. But I highlight and edit what sounds great. I leave out the lonely parts. You don't just wake up one day understanding Vietnamese, knowing where to go and how to avoid getting ripped off.

"But learning to speak [Vietnamese] opened doors for me. My mom was pressing me to find out my biological roots, and at one point I did do a search and went to the town I was born in. I spent two days doing it. I didn't have any hopes or expectations, and I didn't find anything out. But I was comfortable with that. I'd live all of my life not knowing, and just being there helped me come to terms with it. It was closure, I guess you could say."

Having a reason for being there other than just tourism encouraged Tim. As he mastered speaking, he also tackled reading and writing, and he ultimately decided to stay in the country for another two years. He was traveling all over Vietnam by the end of his stay, performing many different tasks for the agency. "That was one of the highlights," he said. "I'd have lunch in the North and dinner in the South and breakfast in Bangkok the next morning."

Although Tim considered getting married and staying forever, the urge to come back home was much stronger. "I wanted to have some kind of foundation," he said. "I wanted to finish college. I knew it was something I had to do."

With so much experience under his belt, it was easy for Tim to get accounting jobs when he returned. He took advantage of all the work available to him, since he had run up a couple thousand dollars of credit card debt during his last year in Vietnam, even though he was earning a small stipend by then. He went back to Maryland to resume his education with classes at the University of Maryland—College Park to earn credits toward his accounting degree.

Socially, things are different for Tim now. "The majority of my friends are Asian, and the women I date are all Asian," he said. "But I like being able to walk both worlds. I know the American way now *and* what it's like for Asians. I can eat in a Ruby Tuesday's on a Tuesday and a Vietnamese restaurant on Wednesday and feel equally comfortable in both."

For more information . . .

See General Resources, Volunteer/Community Service, Volunteer/
Community Service Abroad, page 240.

Randy Lewis
COLLEGE OF WOOSTER
Worked on a boat with environmental activists

Randy Lewis first cut his teeth as an environmental activist on some troublemaking brownies.

"I was a bad, rotten kid. One time in middle school, my friend and I made brownies with a laxative in them and brought them to school to leave for all the teachers. We started bragging right away, and word spread. We got called into the principal's office, and the brownies were sitting there on his desk.

"We told him that the whole thing had been a joke, and that they were just regular brownies. He said in that case we had a choice: we could eat the entire plate of brownies, or he would call our parents and tell them about the joke. So we ate the entire plate, and spent the whole rest of the day in the bathroom."

After several similar stunts, Randy's parents decided he would be better off in boarding school. During his senior year, Randy's boarding school required each student to complete a month-long project before they graduated. "At the time, I had been reading a book about marine mammals. I decided to look further into it, and through my school I was able to go to the Woods Hole Oceanographic Institution in Massachusetts."

Working at Woods Hole opened Randy's eyes to a number of environmental issues that affected marine wildlife. "It was there that I first heard of the Sea Shepherd Conservation Society. A lot of people thought that they were terrorists, blowing up fishing boats and giving a bad name to the environmental movement. I was thinking, 'Wow, cool. These people are actually doing something.' I started reading a lot of environmental magazines and anything I could get my hands on about the Sea Shepherds."

Randy discovered that the Sea Shepherds referred to themselves as a marine mammal conservation society. They owned a boat, which had gone on campaigns to fight the destruction of marine wildlife.

"I learned that they don't injure people, but they do sink ships after getting everyone off. To me, when someone is fishing using illegal or harmful methods, sinking their boat is just like taking a gun away from a person who is about to shoot someone. Violence is hurting another sentient being, not destroying property."

When it came time to apply to college, Randy borrowed a page from the laxative brownie fallout. "I stuck a roll of toilet paper into the typewriter and wrote my college application essay on it. I wrote about a guy who got stuck in the bathroom and had to eat tubes of toothpaste to stay alive. Some of my friends were applying to the College of Wooster in Ohio, so I applied there, and I guess it worked."

Randy arrived at Wooster and found that it was a lot like boarding school, minus the rules. "I did a lot of partying. It was a fun year. I didn't have any real clear goals in mind academically."

After a brief flirtation with being a music major, Randy settled on English. "I saw it as being the most flexible. I thought that maybe I could become a writer about environmental issues, but I was still basically floating around and going through the motions.

"By my sophomore year, I began to think more about what I was going to do when I graduated. I realized that I wasn't getting anything out of school, and I thought it would be a good idea for me to get out into the real world for a while."

Randy's parents were not averse to him spending some time away from the classroom, but they didn't want him sitting in their living room all year either. "They gave me a deadline to figure something out. The deadline was the good, healthy push I needed.

"I decided to call up Sea Shepherds just to check. They sent me this whole crazy application. They wanted to know if I had any police or detective experience, or if I had ever been in the FBI. They've been infiltrated before, so they were worried, I think. They also asked me if I had my own gas mask. I found out later that no one needs to bring his own gas mask. They just ask that to weed people out.

"I answered, 'No, no, no,' to every question, thinking I had no chance. I didn't hear anything back, so I called up and I actually ended up talking to the captain, Paul Watson. He told me that the ship was down in Norfolk, Virginia, and that I should feel free to go down and take a look.

"I kind of misinterpreted him to mean that I was on the boat. He probably thought I would take one look, get scared, and leave. But I threw all my stuff into the car, drove on down, and got on board. I told the four people working on the ship that the captain had sent me down, and I went to work cleaning the boat and painting.

"The captain came down right before the ship was scheduled to leave. It takes a lot to faze him. He talked to the crew about me, and then just said, 'Okay, you're on.' I found out later that they had a stack of applications three feet high. The whole application process is unnecessary. What you need to do is go to it and show them you're a hard worker. Luckily, that's what I did."

The Sea Shepherds are supported by many thousands of members, some of whom are wealthy industrialists who donate large sums of money anonymously. The donations go partly toward feeding the crews and maintaining the ships. It's a large task, considering they burn tens of thousands of dollars in diesel fuel alone on each campaign.

The ship's first destination was the Bahamas. "The captain always keeps the location of the campaign a secret, to prevent media leaks. I thought we were going up to Iceland to sink whaling boats, so I was excited to find out that we were going south instead," Randy said.

"We were [on] a very intimidating ship. The boat is all black, and on the side is a huge steel I-beam sharpened to a point that sticks out from the side. We call that the can opener, and we use it to ram ships. We had a water cannon on board that used to be connected to huge barrels of government-issued custard. We also had butyric acid to throw onto other ships, which is super-stinky stuff.

"We had Kevlar helmets and vests, in case people start[ed] shooting at us, and we had guns on board. Before I was on, they had knives thrown at them by Japanese drift-netters. It's for real. When you head out, you know you might not be coming back, and they outline that to you very clearly before you leave."

The ship sailed to Key West to refuel before setting out on Randy's first wildlife-protection campaign. "We were planning to hunt some 'purse-seiners' off of Mexico. They are tuna fishermen, and tuna tend to hang out under pods of dolphins. These guys find the dolphins and then wrap a huge net around the entire pod. Dolphins are pretty much blind, so [the fishermen] set off underwater explosives to deafen [the dolphins] so they don't move, and the tuna stay put. Then they pull the net in like the drawstrings of a purse.

"They end up pulling in lots of dolphin as well as tuna. The monofilament nets catch the fins of some of the dolphins and tear them off. Dolphins tend to live and hunt in social groups, so even those that get away by themselves starve."

After traveling through the Panama Canal, Randy's ship encountered an even worse sight while sailing north off the coast of Costa Rica. "Boats in protected waters were catching dolphins and cutting them up to throw back in the water as bait for [a] shark. They would catch the shark, cut its fin off, throw the shark back in the water, and send the fin to Japan for shark's fin soup, which is supposed to be an aphrodisiac.

"They were in wooden ships, so if we rammed them, they would have splintered apart. So we threw grappling hooks at them, took their nets away, and threw rum bottles full of butyric acid at them. One drop in an office building can cause the whole place to be evacuated, so they weren't going anywhere for a while. We alerted the Costa Rican government, and they were really thankful. They actually asked us to stay and keep patrolling, but we told them no, we had things to do."

The ship sailed north once more and eventually encountered not Mexican but American purse-seiners. "This was supposedly a dolphin-safe tuna company, and they were so blatant. We went in to try to ram them, but they were faster than we were. We had a smaller, faster ship with us that was able to go in and get really good pictures, though.

"For every one boat you ram, there are hundreds more. We were one tiny ship up against an armada of destruction. But when you get footage like we did, that's something that will get on TV. You'll be sitting in a bar and you'll see it, and say, 'What the hell? Who is that?' That's how widespread change can happen.

"That was one thing that the captain taught me. He is really media-savvy."

The ship docked in Southern California for a few weeks and then set out on its longest campaign since Randy had come on board. "We were going up to the North Pacific to confront some Japanese drift-netters. They lay out thirty-five to forty miles of net. It's monofilament net, so the birds and the fish can't see it, and anything that touches it gets caught. It's not fishing. They're raping the ocean, and it's a sick, sick thing.

"We were up near the Aleutian Islands, and we were going to search until the fuel ran out. The Pacific is much bigger than the Caribbean, so we were in an even worse situation trying to find these boats, but after several false calls, we found them.

"We were a few miles away from them, and we started pulling in their net as they were laying it out. Their nets cost about $1 million apiece, so one of our goals was always to try to get their net, in addition to ramming their ship. But we hadn't foreseen the fact that their net would get completely stuck on our propeller.

"It was one in the morning, and the swells were hitting our ship. We couldn't go anywhere, and we were in serious trouble, because if the swells got any worse and we couldn't turn the propeller on, the boat would turn and we could capsize and drown.

One of my duties on the boat was chief diver, and I had to go down and clear the propeller. We didn't even have a diving knife. I just grabbed a steak knife from the kitchen. Someone came down with me to hold a light, and I got in the cage that held the propeller, which was about as big as I am. The boat was bucking so bad that the propeller was coming out of the water, and I kept slamming my head against the hull. The light was bobbing up and down, and I basically had to do the whole thing by feel.

"I finally got it clear, and then I got caught in the monofilament. It's like quicksand. The more you struggle, the more you get snagged, and then the other guy got caught too. I didn't even panic, I just figured I was going to die. Thank God we both did the right thing. We were able to relax and float up to the surface, and they came in with the small boat and cut us free. It was the closest brush with death I've ever had."

They managed to pull in a few miles of net that night, and the next morning they moved in to ram the ship. "We had made radio contact and told them that what they were doing was illegal. We had deliberately timed the campaign to coincide with an international moratorium on drift-netting, but the United Nations doesn't do anything. We were the only ones out there enforcing it.

"We circled them a few times, made a few rushes at them, and turned away at the last moment, just toying with them. Then we moved in and called them on the radio and said, 'Prepare to be rammed.' It was going to be a direct hit, really hard, but as we were about to hit them, some guy comes out on their deck walking toward where we were going to hit them. We turned away at the last moment, and it ended up being a sort of glancing blow, but the crunch was still pretty incredible."

Once again the Sea Shepherds were outrun, as the Japanese ship retreated. Randy and the crew turned around to head for Canada, but they were stopped almost immediately. "The Japanese had told the American government that we were throwing Molotov cocktails at their ship, so we were intercepted by the Coast Guard. Some people came on board and interrogated every one of us. I think they were from the FBI, but they never identified themselves. They started asking me all these questions, like whether I was an anarchist, whether I believed in God, and whether I thought there should be a revolution. I said, 'Look, I'm just out here trying to protect marine wildlife.'"

Randy managed to make it back to North America without getting arrested, and he toyed with the idea of not returning to school. "We were going to go up and sink whalers in Iceland, but that campaign was delayed. It was close to September at that point, and I had already finished two years of school. I knew if I didn't go back then, I probably never would.

"Coming back was really hard. I'd been out at sea for a year, living such an adventure, and each day at school seemed so boring. Every person seemed so boring, just the sameness of them all. I thought I had made the wrong choice.

"Then all of a sudden it happened, real quick. I realized that what I really wanted to do was change my major to something more environmentally focused, maybe environmental science. I looked into it and found that nothing like it existed at the college.

"So I started talking to a biology professor, and she was a big help. She told me that if I wanted to do it on my own, I would have to take certain classes. I got the degree requirements from other schools that had an environmental science major, and I developed a program of my own.

"I was going to have to take biology, chemistry, geology, and then take political science classes to balance it out. It was an incredibly burdensome schedule, but I realized, if I was going to be there, why not make the best of it? I knew by then that I wanted to go into environmental work, so I just focused on that, and I worked harder than I had ever worked in school before.

"I came across a lot of opposition. The school was going through some cutbacks, and I think the last thing they needed was someone designing a major that other people would want to do, which would lead into having to create another department. Some professors didn't think it was a serious enough pursuit, and some others didn't think I would get enough depth. But I went on and graduated, and I was the first person ever to graduate from my school with an environmental science major. Near the end, people came up to me to find out how they could do the same thing. I left a legacy."

While Randy believes that more people should consider taking time off, he said that any activist should think hard about what he or she is prepared to endure for a cause. "There are so many people I would not recommend Sea Shepherds to. There were people who came on the boat at one stop and got right off at the next. Some people should be working in Washington talking to politicians. You've got to do whatever your calling is.

"It was a hard life out there, but there is nothing like sitting out on the front deck when a pod of dolphins starts riding the bow wave of your ship. I looked down at them once, and one turned on its side, waved with his flipper, and jumped up to the point where I could nearly touch him. Almost as if to say, 'Hey, thanks for what you're doing.' Experiences like that, I wouldn't trade for the world."

For more information . . .

www.seashepherd.org—Read about the history of the Sea Shepherds, and recent events, and enlist for the next voyage.

www.marinecareers.net—Provides links to a wide range of marine careers and the people in them, personal anecdotes, news coverage, and organizations.

www.fguardians.org—"Forest Guardians—Leading the fight to protect and restore the forests, rivers, grasslands, wildlife and wilderness of the Southwest." Provides many links to environmental information, organizations, and activism.

Cory Mason
CENTENARY COLLEGE
Volunteered for Habitat for Humanity

While Cory Mason's friends were busily filling out college applications, he was on the way to setting a record for skipping the most days of school and still graduating.

Cory had begun high school full of enthusiasm, lettering on the varsity swim team as a freshman and eventually qualifying for national tournaments. "Any self-discipline I've ever had comes from swimming," Cory observed. "Practice is grueling; you go back and forth over and over again. There's no change of scenery, and you can't really talk to anybody."

Cory attended a public high school in Racine, Wisconsin, with 2,400 students. He was in the international baccalaureate program, which he described as "almost a school within a school." IB programs usually consist of an accelerated, intensive course of study for talented students, and they can be found in many countries. "Out of 600 kids in my graduating class," Cory said, "50 were in the IB program. We had the best teachers in each department, which was an unfair advantage, but we had a lot more homework, too."

Early on in high school, many of Cory's friends came from swimming. "There were three or four of us who got on the varsity team freshman year. That was great, but they hazed the hell out of us. One time they tied up one of my friends naked in a towel bag, threw him into the pool during girls' swim class, and when he got out of the bag, there he was, stark naked. It was awful."

Because of the swim meets Cory participated in every weekend, the Mason family could no longer go to church on Sundays. "Sometimes we'd go fifteen weekends in a row where we'd be at swim meets every weekend. It consumed our entire life. My dad looked at that time the family spent together as our church. He firmly believed that religion didn't necessarily have to take place in church, and he was glad that his family was together and that his kids were doing something constructive."

Swimming started to wear on Cory at the end of high school, and a shoulder injury increased his ambivalence about the sport. "It dawned on me: Was it really worth it to work hard seven months at a crack, without a break, in order to drop my time by half a second?

"I went through a period where I just felt real blasé about everything. It drove my parents up the wall. Some people at my school went through a senior slump; I had a senior plummet. The last two years of high school seemed to last forever. I wanted to be grown-up and have real responsibilities."

Like all his friends, Cory went through the motions of applying to colleges during his senior year. As the time approached to make a decision, however, he became certain that going straight to college was not for him. "It just seemed that everybody I knew was going to the University of Wisconsin at Madison. A lot of kids from my school go there and only hang out with the kids they knew from high school. That just seems so limiting, and I was really scared that was going to happen to me."

In the midst of a difficult senior year, Cory was also going through a yearlong confirmation program with his priest, Father Bruce. "Father Bruce was really cool; he's the only priest I know who wears an earring. The main group met on Sunday nights and we had a smaller group that met on Tuesday nights to discuss things in greater depth.

"Our small group studied the vow of nonviolence, not just physical violence, but also violence of the heart and mind. We are in a society that is constantly bombarded with violence. Our entire legal system is adversarial; our political system is confrontational. I was learning more through confirmation than I was in school."

Cory's confirmation program also included community service. "During Christmas, we were each given a family that we had to raise money for. We organized a Polar Bear plunge. We ran into Lake Michigan on January 14. The water was freezing, and they had an ambulance on hand. A couple of us were crazy enough to swim out to the buoy and back. We got on the front page of the newspaper. It's now become a tradition, and we bring in a couple thousand dollars every year."

Cory recalls telling Father Bruce that he was not ready to go to college. "I had heard so many stories about the kids at Madison. They go up there, party all the time, don't go to class, and flunk out their first semester. What a waste. And I tell you, that would have been me."

When Cory asked Father Bruce if he knew anything about missionary work, Father Bruce gave him some booklets. Unfortunately many of the organizations wanted only people who were at least twenty-one years old. "You would think, with something like missionary work, that when someone asks to volunteer they'd do everything they could to encourage that person and help him or her set it up. It was the most bureaucratic thing I've ever been involved with."

Cory's parents wondered what he was doing. "I had to explain to them why we had this astronomical phone bill, including calls to Venezuela. I told them I was thinking about taking time off and investigating the possibilities of some kind of religiously inspired community service in South America. My dad said, 'Cory, I know so many kids who took time off and never came back. It's rough out there in the real world.' I said, 'Yeah, yeah, you're right.' But with my mom, who knew I was not ready for college, I convinced him to give me the benefit of the doubt."

Cory applied to work for Habitat for Humanity and was accepted in June. Habitat for Humanity is an organization dedicated to providing affordable housing for low-income families. Habitat now has affiliates in eighty-three countries and chapters in all fifty U.S. states.

Habitat gave Cory a choice of three sites: Ontario, Canada; Waco, Texas; and Savannah, Georgia. "I decided on Savannah because they let me be project manager, and the fact that it was ten miles away from the ocean was real appealing. The town is beautiful, right on the Savannah River."

Cory's duties as project manager included helping build houses, overseeing and managing the construction sites, and training the volunteers and recipient families. In return for his services, he was given room, board, and a stipend of twenty dollars a week. "It was rough getting by on twenty dollars a week," he said. "And if you wanted to use the truck, you had to put gas in it. It was an old, beat-up Chevy truck that gets something like eight miles to the gallon, and you had to drive all the way into town and all the way back."

Cory was in charge of a project to build fifty-two new houses on a thirteen-acre site in rural Savannah. "I had never built a house before, nor had I lifted a hammer to do anything aside from hang a picture on a wall." But Cory caught on quickly. He figured out a lot on his own, and he also had two teachers: the other project manager at his site, and a construction superintendent hired by Habitat.

Habitat builds houses that vary in size, depending on the needs of the family moving in. The houses come with heat and central air, a stove, and a refrigerator. Habitat then sells the houses at a low rate to families who have contributed "sweat equity" to the project and gives them a mortgage with interest that's below market rates. The organization is able to financially break even through private donations of money, material, and labor from people like Cory.

Cory found it inspiring to work with people from various backgrounds. "The thing about working construction is, nobody wears nice clothes. People would show up in jeans and T-shirts. Most of the rich people who volunteered from the nearby retirement community didn't know much about construction, and neither did most of the recipients. That was one of the neatest things about working there: seeing people from all different walks of life coming together and deciding they were going to put up a wall that afternoon."

The most difficult part of Cory's stay in Savannah came toward the end of February. "Habitat International had what's called the Spring Break Challenge. They go to college campuses and recruit groups to work at a site for a week. I was a little worried about telling these twenty-two-year-olds what to do. I thought they were going to say, 'You're just a little punk out of high school. What are you talking about?' But when it came right down to it, most of them had no clue about construction, and I did."

Cory didn't have a chance to party like a college student with those who came down to volunteer. "We went forty-three days straight without a day off. It was rough, because at night in the dormitories they'd say, 'We want to see what Savannah's like; can you show us around the town?' By the time I left, I could have applied to be a tour guide for the summer."

When Cory left Savannah, he was able to get a job working construction in Racine. "It was great because I was learning a trade. I learned all about roofing, Sheetrock, electricity, and a little bit about plumbing."

After working in Racine for the summer, Cory enrolled at Centenary College, a small Methodist-affiliated liberal arts school in Shreveport, Louisiana.

"Coming back to Racine was good. I had been at odds with my parents when I was living at home my senior year. When I came back, they were actually glad to have me. Earlier, my dad had been kind of worried. His eldest son, who was supposed to go off to college, was doing something kind of wacky. But by the time I left for Centenary, he was actually proud of what I had done and would tell people at work about it.

"For a long time I took great pride in being discontent with everything around me. There was a certain appeal to that, being a pain in the ass. That's not to say that I don't still question things that go on around me. The biggest change, though, is that now I'm at peace with myself.

"I see kids in college who could be learning a lot more by just taking a year off and working somewhere. You learn to pay your bills. You have to make sure you know where your next meal is coming from. You also learn that if you don't have an education, you can't get a stable job. I didn't like scraping by on twenty dollars a week, and I don't want to scrape for my next meal the rest of my life.

"You can't learn that without leaving school. In college, you just live in your dorm room, all your meals are cooked for you, and it's pretty simple. All you have to do is show up."

In fact, Cory was so sure of the value of his time off that he did it again before he finished school, taking a year to work as an organizer and lobbyist in Connecticut. Eventually, he ended up back in Wisconsin, went to work for a local political candidate, and signed up for classes at the University of Wisconsin (the very institution that he so dreaded during his senior year in high school).

What followed was a series of political jobs in the state that never would have been possible had he not taken time off. "There isn't a single job that I have ever been offered that wasn't a direct result of the time I took off to try something new," he said. "More importantly, there isn't a single experience I've had taking time off that hasn't contributed positively to the person I am today. It was revealing to me that because of my practical experience, my education was a secondary consideration in all of the jobs I have been offered so far. I watched many friends graduate with undergraduate and master's degrees struggle to find employment in something that they liked.

"There were times when I would wonder where I would be had I done the traditional route through school. But now that it's all behind me, I couldn't be happier with my decisions.

"I'm not suggesting that taking time off is right for everyone. But it certainly isn't wrong for everyone either. So many people I know aren't even working in the field in which they received a degree. If that's to be the norm, people are going to need different experiences and skills to be competitive. People are going to need those different experiences to be happy." Today Cory is the government relations director for the Wisconsin Federation of Teachers, which represents teachers and other public employees in the education field.

"I love it," he said. "I get to spend my days debating public policy on issues that I truly care about, and I get to participate in one of the world's greatest activities: representative democracy. What's more, I know I could not be doing what I am doing now had I not been willing to take the road less traveled and try out different things."

For more information . . .

If I Were a Carpenter: Twenty Years of Habitat For Humanity, by Frye Gaillard. John F. Blair, 1996. The history, mission, success, and future of Habitat for Humanity, all told in this book.

Love in the Mortar Joints, by Millard Fuller and Diane Scott. New Win Publishing, 1980. The story of Habitat for Humanity, written by one of the original founders of the organization.

www.habitat.org—Official website of Habitat for Humanity, where you can sign up for a Global Village volunteer vacation (where you'll help someone somewhere in the world build a house) and e-mail alerts to keep you abreast of Habitat news.

Kara Nelson
UNIVERSITY OF CALIFORNIA AT BERKELEY
Helped start a school in Zimbabwe

Kara Nelson's first chance to explore her interest in developing countries came when she realized that Mexico was right in her own backyard. "One day in high school, I realized that there is this incredibly poor country right next to mine, and I had never been there."

After her graduation from high school in Corvallis, Oregon, Kara and her mother took a three-week trip to Mexico. They traveled Lonely Planet–style, in the spirit of the popular low-budget travel guides published by Lonely Planet Publications. "We stayed in hotels where the Mexicans stayed and took regular Mexican buses. At the time I thought what we were doing was crazy, that we were crossing the boundaries of traditional tourism. Of course, when I look back on it now, it's pretty tame compared to my subsequent traveling experiences."

Before she had another chance to travel in a developing country, Kara enrolled at the University of California at Berkeley. She was excited to begin school and had no fear of getting lost in the crowd. A strong science background in high school made a physics major at Berkeley a likely choice for her.

Classes were not as difficult as she thought they would be, which turned out to be a mixed blessing. "I just crammed before each test and got A's or B's. It took me a long time to recover from the bad study habits I developed."

A growing interest in radical politics and an active social life also affected Kara's attitude toward her studies. "There was just so much going on all the time. Every single day, there were protests on campus. There was an organization for every cause that you can imagine, and for causes that you've never heard of, even if you think you've heard of everything.

"I felt like America was damaging the entire rest of the world, and that most people didn't even know it. I grew up with this great life of incredible material affluence, in comparison with how most people around the world live. Unfortunately I had no knowledge of the impact my life was having on the rest of the planet.

"At the same time, my physics classes just started getting less and less relevant to any of my life interests. The people in my classes were really lame. I just couldn't relate to most of them."

Feeling frustrated with both her academics and her extracurricular activities, Kara began to explore other options. Her first idea, a formal study-abroad program, did not meet her needs. "I was really sick of school and didn't know what I wanted from it. So, if I was going to take time off, I certainly didn't want to be in school."

Kara had always wanted to learn French, which inspired her to look into studying abroad, specifically in West Africa. Her interest in Africa combined with a desire to volunteer in a development organization led her to the former British colony of Zimbabwe.

When exploring her options, Kara found some of the most valuable information and resources right on Berkeley's campus. "All colleges have international connections. There are so many people around who have been to other countries, whether for academic reasons, [for] personal interests, or because that's where they're from. You have to reach out and talk to those people."

Kara still needed to earn enough money to finance her trip, so she went back to Corvallis, home of Oregon State University. "I ended up putting up flyers all over the OSU campus in all the science departments. The flyers said I had lab experience and that I just needed to work for a little while. I found two jobs in two different labs. I worked at one in the morning and at the other in the afternoon."

Kara's hard work paid off, and she was soon on her way to Harare, Zimbabwe. When she stepped off the plane, it took her a moment to get her bearings.

"There I was, trying to figure out how to get to a city that I couldn't even see, and two women walked up to me and said, 'Wow, we really like your shoes.'"

Kara told them that she had come to Zimbabwe for four months and hoped to volunteer for an aid organization. Because it had been difficult to make arrangements with aid organizations from home, Kara hoped she would be able to find a volunteer opportunity once she arrived. She also explained that she planned to stay at the youth hostel in Harare. "'You can't stay at the youth hostel for four months,' they said. 'What are you thinking?'"

Kara shared a cab ride into the city with the two women and dropped her belongings off at their apartment. The Zimbabweans then took Kara to meet two British men who were working with a social service organization named Toc-H.

"Toc-H ran a number of racially mixed hostels in Harare, mostly for old white army veterans and young black men from rural areas who were studying in the city. In return for living there, the hostel's residents were required to do social work," Kara explained.

On her first day in Zimbabwe, the two British men took Kara to an orphanage for children who were missing one or more limbs. "The orphanage was out in a high-density suburb—a euphemism for slum—and there were kids without legs dragging themselves around on the ground and kids without arms who couldn't feed themselves. We threw them a party, with soda and cake, guitars, singing, dancing, and hanging out. It was me, the two British guys, the two Zimbabwean women I'd met at the airport, and a bunch of Zimbabweans who lived at the hostel."

Kara's friends from the airport quickly found her a place to live. "I returned to their apartment and they said, 'Oh, we arranged for you to live with our friend Anne.' Anne was an incredibly empowered woman in her own way. She went to vocational training school to become a lithographer [a type of printing] and was the first woman in Zimbabwe ever to go through that training program."

When she looked into finding a teaching job, Kara ran into a ferocious bureaucracy. "Even though they desperately needed science teachers, at any level, in any school, I found so many things getting in the way."

She also looked into volunteering with one of the many nongovernmental organizations (NGOs) operating in Zimbabwe. NGOs often build infrastructure and provide basic human services in countries where the government itself isn't doing those things. "None of the NGOs wanted me. They need an incredible amount of time to initiate a volunteer into their organizations and to actually get you to the point where you can be useful doing something. I realized that you can't just go over there and then all of a sudden make great things happen. You need to make a serious commitment and it takes a long time."

Kara's persistence paid off, however, and she finally discovered a unique volunteer opportunity. After the country's independence from British rule, Zimbabwe's mostly rural, extended family–based society was under strain from increasing urbanization and industrialization. "Because of the independence war, a lot of people were left homeless and landless and familyless, and they all started migrating to the city. A mass education policy in rural areas increased the number of people who migrated from the countryside to look for better jobs in the city."

The British people Kara met upon arriving in Harare put her in contact with a community of homeless people who had taken over some sprawling fields on the edge of town. "The squatters went around to different service organizations, especially churches, and got them to donate things, like blankets, clothing, and black plastic to use for tents. They would also get restaurants to give them food once a week. The area was basically a shantytown. The squatters elected a group of people to represent them in their lobbying effort to get the government to give them agricultural land on which to resettle. The Lancaster Agreement, which said there would be no land distribution in the first ten years following independence, had expired.

"They also decided to start their own school. The kids couldn't go to a regular school, since they didn't have a permanent address. So I offered to help start the school. It was super-informal. We would sit under a big tree. We had a broken blackboard that they had gotten somewhere, with a big crack through the middle of it. Sometimes we had chalk or pencils and paper.

"When I arrived in the morning, all the kids would see me and come running out to hug me. 'Kara's here, Kara's here.' Everyone would get all excited and the adults would say, 'Schooltime, it's schooltime.' Adults who didn't know English would come and sit in on my classes."

Kara's students ranged in age from near-infants to girls fifteen or sixteen years old. "The oldest boys were nine or ten, because by the time they were teenagers, most boys would go into town all day, either to beg for spare change or to wash windows.

In her spare time, Kara was learning to play the *mbira,* a Zimbabwean thumb piano, and studying the Shona language at the local adult college. As for whether it was hard to make friends, Kara says, "I was more plagued by having too many people who wanted to be my friend."

Kara ended her time in Zimbabwe with some solo travel to nearby Malawi, passing through war-ravaged Mozambique on the way. "It's so sketchy," she said. "I can't believe I did that."

She traveled what is known as the "gun run," where each day the armies from Zimbabwe and Malawi would escort a convoy of trucks through the Tete corridor. The corridor runs through Mozambique and connects Zimbabwe with Malawi. "The convoy goes through once a day in each direction. Anyone can go through, but no one does it besides truck drivers and a few crazy people in private cars.

"On the way there, I ended up getting a ride with this totally racist white South African family. They were scared South Africa was being taken over by the blacks, so they were going to go and live in the bush in Malawi and make their own world. Super-weird.

"The whole road was completely blown up, because land mines had been planted everywhere. The saddest part was the town of Tete, which was completely cut off from the rest of the world because of the war. There's absolutely nothing there, just thousands of starving people.

"There were hundreds and hundreds of people lining the streets when the convoy arrived, coming up to you. They were trying to sell you things that they had gotten from some aid organization, like men's button-down shirts, which were of no use to them. They needed food or fuel; they didn't need a button-down shirt."

On the way back, Kara rode with a truck driver. "The convoy was scheduled to leave at dawn but was postponed by policemen and soldiers gesticulating madly. I found out later that the day before, the convoy had been attacked. No one on the convoy had been killed, but the army went after the rebel soldiers and killed four of them. The truck driver told me, 'No big deal, I do this all the time.' I thought, 'Oh, my God. I'm going to die.'"

One of Kara's biggest shocks upon returning to the United States was rediscovering America's aversion to talking about race. "In Zimbabwe, it's a given that they live in a racist society. The white people discriminated against the black people. It's true, it happened, it still exists, and it's okay to talk about it. In the United States, we have this false image that everything is hunky-dory and that we don't live in a racist society anymore."

When she came back to Berkeley, Kara tried to pick up where she had left off, enrolling in the second semester of quantum mechanics and working to complete her physics major. "We spent five weeks trying to get an approximate solution to one equation for the motion of one atom. I started thinking that what I really wanted to do was work in developing countries and work with the environment."

Kara decided to become an environmental engineer and changed her major to biophysics. After graduating, she researched international climate change and decided to enroll in graduate school. She picked up a master's degree in environmental engineering at the University of Washington and completed her Ph.D. in the same topic at the University of California at Davis.

Along the way, she returned to Mexico, where she sampled ponds as part of an effort to better understand how to treat municipal wastewater and inactivate the eggs of a particularly resilient intestinal parasite.

After Kara's many years of graduate work, Berkeley welcomed her back in 2001, and today she's a professor there and continues to develop technologies that can help improve the infrastructure in developing nations.

For more information . . .

www.ivpsf.com—The International Volunteer Program promotes volunteering in Europe and the United States. The website provides program descriptions, resource links, former participants' feedback, and general program information.

www.unv.org—Official website for UN Volunteer Program offers resource links, news coverage of global volunteering efforts, and lists of activities and partnerships around the globe.

www.crossculturalsolutions.org—Website listing global volunteer/work abroad opportunities in China, Peru, Russia, Ghana, Costa Rica, and India. Also provides resource links to other volunteer programs and general volunteering advice.

Burke Olsen
BRIGHAM YOUNG UNIVERSITY
Spent two years on a Mormon mission in Scotland and
a semester working on the 2002 Winter Olympics
torch relay

For some, taking time off from college has always been part of the plan. And after seeing what a great experience it is, a few even choose to do it again before collecting their undergraduate degrees.

Burke Olsen grew up in Belmont, Massachusetts, with leave takers constantly passing through his living room. When Burke was four years old, his father became Massachusetts mission president for the Mormon Church, overseeing the evangelical activities of approximately 150 to 200 young people at a time.

As each missionary in the region began his or her eighteen- to twenty-four-month stint taking time off from college, he or she would pass through the Olsen home and sit around the dinner table with the Olsen clan. "Being around [the young missionaries] and looking up to them created a desire in me to be a missionary too," he said.

Growing up the youngest of five children, Burke often heard the stories of his older siblings who had already been on missions. By the time he enrolled at Brigham Young University, he was already preparing for his own journey and wondering where the Church would send him. "It's a mystery," Burke said. "We really don't know where we'll go. You can say if you'd like to learn a language and how successful you think you'd be. I did say I was interested [in learning a foreign language] and I ended up in Scotland, where the Scottish brogue made it sound quite unlike the English that I grew up with."

With his supposedly deep knowledge of what missionary work involved, Burke was certain he'd hit the ground running once he arrived across the Atlantic. "I was very confident. Probably overconfident," he said. "I found myself very discouraged, very homesick, and very overwhelmed at the long hours. We only had half a day off each week, which was something I hadn't known. Having been in New England [with all of those missionaries marching through the living room] and having had older brothers [who had gone on missions themselves], I couldn't believe that I didn't know that."

Burke's father, well aware of the emotional roller-coaster ride his son was embarking on, had slipped a letter into Burke's suitcase. "He said, 'You're probably feeling discouraged right now, and that's just normal,'" Burke said. "Just having my father tell me that made me feel like I wasn't weak and I wasn't bad."

Burke's parents supported him financially, too, sending $375 each month to the church to go toward the traditional uniformlike clothes, books, and lodging. "We lived in flats, with either two or four to a flat, and we shared bedrooms," Burke said. "They were decent, depending on how well the missionaries before you took care of them. Still, when you share such compact quarters with three other people, it's amazing what becomes a luxury."

But with little time on his hands, Burke didn't have much of a chance to wonder what sort of recreational pursuits or European travel he was missing out on. Training began in earnest as soon as he arrived, as he learned more about how to present the six lessons that missionaries use to teach people about the Mormon religion. "We did role-playing," Burke said. "But nothing can quite prepare you for what it's like to approach a Scotsman on the road or at his front door."

To help ease him in, Burke's mission president paired him with a more experienced companion. The presidents do this with every new missionary so that the new arrivals can see how others who have been in the field for a while do their work. Chris was Burke's companion, and he had a great effect on Burke.

"As a new missionary, you put so much of who you are into how people are reacting to what you want to teach them," Burke explained. "It was hard for me, being so enthusiastic about finally being a missionary, with my name on my chest and the name of the savior next to mine. It made me feel a great responsibility. So when people would tell me no, that they didn't want to hear what I had to tell them, it was very hard.

"Chris taught me how to love people. I had to learn the lesson that people weren't rejecting me. They were rejecting my message. He loved them just the same, and I never heard him say a negative thing about people who wouldn't let us into their homes or had terrible problems that would be obstacles to them joining the church."

Some of the obstacles were quite large, though. "Many times they were lifestyle-oriented," Burke said. "It was tough if people were living together and weren't married or if they had addictions. Tobacco and alcohol were the greatest challenges we had," as Mormons abstain from drinking and smoking. "We couldn't do much other than encourage them to go to Alcoholics Anonymous or to enter the program the Church had to help people quit smoking," Burke added. "We didn't go into pubs, either. That was one of the rules. I can't imagine that it would be a great place to teach people. Someone nursing their lager probably won't take a copy of the Book of Mormon while all their other friends are in there with them."

Since missionaries are often knocking on doors during daylight hours, they're more likely to run into people with substance-abuse problems. "When people are home during the day, it may mean that they're down on their luck and discouraged," he said. "After a while, I'd been there long enough to know when someone was drunk and that they would not remember anything we had taught them, even if they did let us in to their homes."

Still, Burke and his various companions during his two-year mission managed to reach some frequent drinkers. "One of my companions, Preston, set up a follow-up visit during the middle of the day on our one precious half-day off," Burke recalled. "But we went, and she was sober, and we had one of the greatest discussions I'd ever had with anybody. She felt the spirit and we felt the spirit, and five lessons later she was baptized. So the lesson I learned from Preston is that sacrifice brings blessings."

Burke is quick to point out, however, that he didn't spend all of his time attempting to tend to the needs of people with substance-abuse problems. In fact, some of the most rewarding work involved reaching out to Mormons who had fallen out of touch with the Church. "If it was raining, we'd go visit them," he explained. They were the ones most likely to allow him and his partner to come inside, where it was dry. "Some of the greatest successes that I had, that I couldn't have anticipated, came from helping people who had fallen away become active again."

But it's the cold-calling—the door-to-door, meet-on-the-street aspect of missionary work—for which Mormons are most well known. Burke spent a good chunk of his time doing that, too. While he was lucky to be in a country where citizens are not frightened by in-person solicitations, he and his fellow missionaries did have one disadvantage working against them. "There was a branch of the British police that had uniforms similar to ours," Burke explained. "More than once, people would see us knocking on their doors and would flush their drugs down the toilet."

Burke decided early on that it would be a mistake to set quotas for the number of baptisms and conversions he inspired. "I did it on purpose," he explained. "I didn't want to think about the number itself but about the individuals who touched my life and whose lives I touched."

Nevertheless, he was discouraged at first by his slow progress. "It was hard work, and it was slow going," he recalled. "I'd been there almost eleven months before someone I taught was baptized, though the next thirteen months were much more productive. It did send me through a period of self-doubt. I wondered what was wrong with my own life and how I could make myself as worthy of that blessing as possible.

"But we also knew that people have agency in their own lives, and we're not able to change that. The hope is that if we live our own lives correctly, the Lord will lead us to people pure in heart who are looking for our message."

On that note, the Church makes sure each missionary has a partner at all times. Part of the reason for this is so that they can buck each other up and help each other resist temptation, whether it's alcohol or romance. Missionaries are not supposed to date during their two years away, and those who leave boyfriends or girlfriends behind often find that their partners have moved on by the time they return home. "It's part of the lore of missionary life," Burke recalled. "The 'Dear John' letter is oft expected but never desired." Indeed, Burke returned to Utah to find that his previous girlfriend had gotten engaged to someone else.

But nowadays it also makes sense to pair missionaries up for their own protection. "In a climate where Catholic priests have been accused of so much, if you always have two people together, that means there's always a witness," Burke said. "We can be protected not only from doing anything untoward but also from anyone accusing us of doing something inappropriate."

There are other dangers, too; a few years ago, two missionaries were kidnapped in Russia and held for ransom. They were eventually released without being harmed.

During his two years, Burke spent most of his time in the center of Scotland, between Glasgow and Edinburgh, though he worked some on the coast as well. Toward the end of his stay, he had the opportunity to train two new missionaries himself, and he eventually served as the assistant to the mission president, living in his house and accompanying him on his travels around the country.

He also taught a class on journal keeping, something he recommends for anyone spending an extended amount of reflective time away from the classroom. "My great-grandfather had served a mission in Samoa exactly 100 years before me," Burke said. "He kept a journal, and my father sent it to me. His experiences were in some cases similar to mine, and it gave me great strength to know that he'd been through some of the same challenges as I had."

After a brief trip around Scotland with his family, Burke returned home and reenrolled in school. During the semester before he had left for Scotland, Burke spent so much time preparing for his mission that he hadn't gotten very good grades. That changed once he returned. "If nothing else, I learned how to be disciplined, how to become the master of my time," he said.

In fact, he did well enough in his chosen public relations major to attract the attentions of the head of a big public relations firm, Coltrin & Associates, which had been founded by a former spokesman for the Mormon church. Burke interned there one summer, and fifteen months later, the firm's founder asked him to take time off from college to work with the agency to promote the Olympic torch relay that would precede the 2002 Winter Games in Salt Lake City.

Burke initially resisted the urge to leave school once again, at least at first, but he ultimately couldn't pass up the opportunity to be part of something so important in such trying times. "It did give me pause," he explained. "But how could I not take advantage of an opportunity to be part of something so big taking place in my backyard? I jumped at the chance, and I never looked back."

After finishing the winter semester of 2001, Burke joined the Coltrin & Associates team. The agency paid him as if he were an entry-level professional, and he went to work promoting the trip that the torch would take. It started in Greece and traveled to Salt Lake City for the start of the Games. Along the way it would travel by air, but also by road for many hundreds of miles, carried along the way by thousands of people.

One of Burke's biggest responsibilities was to help pick the VIP torch-bearers and communicate the logistics of how, when, and where they'd be carrying the torch. Aretha Franklin was among his favorites, as was Arizona Diamondbacks pitcher Curt Schilling. In recognition of the September 11 attacks, Burke took on the additional task of inviting 100 rescue workers, family members of people who died, and others who had been affected by the tragedy to run with the torch as well.

After making all of these arrangements, he went to Greece to fetch the torch. "Delta gave us a whole plane and some of their best flight attendants," he recalled. "We got there, lit it with the rays of the sun in a special ceremony at the Temple Hera, then flew back eighteen hours later. The torch and several lit lanterns were strapped in their own row of seats, and we had to get special permission from the government to keep them lit while the plane was in the air."

The relay was a massive expedition, parading through forty-six states in sixty-five days, covering 13,500 miles in total. Once Burke had gotten the VIPs under control, he joined the tour for the last three weeks, traveling through many of the western states. "My job was to arrive wherever the torch was going an hour or two ahead of time to line up interviews for the relay spokesperson," he explained. "It was pretty taxing. I was up every day at 6 A.M. and not in bed until midnight, at a different hotel each night." During the games, Burke worked in the main media center, helping reporters from all over the world.

Once he returned to school, Burke realized how relevant his classes were to work in the real world. He hadn't felt that to be true prior to this second period of time off. "From day one I was grateful," he said. "Prior to having work experience, I don't think I would have appreciated how relevant something like statistics is."

More than that, however, the real lesson from working to promote the Olympics came from the sustained exposure to working people with a variety of experience and expertise, the kind that you just can't get in a two-month summer internship. Burke found the range of the experiences that these people brought to bear on their Olympics work inspiring. "I have an understanding now of how diverse and exciting someone's career can be," he said. "The people I worked with had given up all sorts of careers at the top of their fields to dedicate themselves to a good cause, a world cause. I don't think any of them had trouble getting back into long-term jobs after they were done with their work with the Olympics.

"As a college student, you feel this great pressure to narrow your focus, declare a major. If anything, my experience has led me to believe that I don't just have to be one thing. I can have a great and exciting career that passes through many fields."

For more information . . .

www.mormons.org and **www.lds.org**—Official websites of the
Church of Jesus Christ of Latter-day Saints where you can find out
more about missionary work and the doctrine and history of the
Church. You have to be Mormon to serve a Mormon mission, and
your local congregation should be able to explain the application
process to you.

Brendan Robinson
JOHNSON C. SMITH COLLEGE
Enrolled in City Year, a yearlong service program

For Brendan Robinson, *Boyz N the Hood* was not just a movie. It was his life. "Most of my friends came from Cathedral Projects, a housing project in the South End section of Boston. In the beginning we were little shorties, little kids doing little-kid things, like riding bikes together," he said.

This changed at age twelve. That was when Brendan and his friends formed a gang. "We started a group, the little Heath Streets. We were into breakdancing and pretending to be rappers. Then it grew into something I'm not proud to say I was part of. When you gangbang, you have to do a certain amount of criminal activity, called 'dirt.' Once you reach a certain point, you're not a little kid anymore. You're what you call a G, a Gangster, or an OG, an Original Gangster."

Belonging to a gang gave Brendan a tremendous sensation of power. "Gangbanging takes you way beyond acceptance, way beyond love, way beyond colors. It was energy. I could go to a party, and if anyone tried to kick my ass, they would have twenty other guys to deal with. And if it really got ridiculous, I could get on the phone and have everybody down there."

Things began to fall apart when crack and guns hit the neighborhood at the same time. "One day they weren't there, and the next day they were. Not too many people knew it would be a multibillion-dollar business," he said.

A steady and diverse stream of customers came to Brendan in search of crack. "I'd get white guys with a suit and tie on, driving up in a Lexus, risking their lives driving through the projects just so they can get their high.

"Those are the people that would be home reading a newspaper or watching the evening news about the inner city, and say, 'Damn, honey, do you believe what those people are doing?' Just a couple hours earlier, they were doing exactly what they were describing on the news: buying drugs."

When Brendan bumped into his white customers in other parts of the city, most of them ignored him. "Those are the same people who won't give you a job. I've had white people say, 'Hey, buddy, how are you?' when they wanted drugs. On the train, they just turned their head away from me. I thought, 'Next time I see you down in the projects, I'm not going to recognize you, and we'll see how it feels. Probably lonesome and scary.'"

The deaths of people close to him began to take a toll on Brendan's psyche. "I spent a lot of time talking with my best friend, Randy, about how we wished we were never in this life to begin with.

"I remember waiting for the bus to go to school one day during the spring of my freshman year. It was 6:30 A.M. on March 21. Randy walked by and said, 'Yo, B, why don't you hook school with me and chill with these girls I'm going to go meet now?' He wasn't a school-going kind of guy."

Brendan told Randy he would catch up with him after school, and they gave each other a parting hug. "Then a car pulled around that had already passed by a few times. There was a kid in there that Randy had shot at a party two months earlier during a fight over a girl. He had a big gauze bandage on his neck.

"I heard four gunshots. I started running down the street, and I knew it was Randy. It felt like someone had stuck a pin in my heart, and all my feelings went numb."

As he sprinted toward Randy, Brendan ran into the person with the gauze patch on his neck. "When he saw me coming, he took his gun out and pointed it at me. When he pulled back the handle, there were no bullets left.

"I wasn't thinking at the time about how close I came to dying. I was thinking about Randy. He was on a porch in a prone position with blood everywhere. He looked really cold and was shaking a lot."

Brendan held Randy in his arms until the paramedics arrived. "Before they put him in the ambulance, the last thing he said to me was 'I love you.' His parents were dead. I was the only person left in the world who cared about him. Randy was DOA at the hospital," he said.

Brendan started to think about doing things differently. "I remember sitting in the dark for hours and crying. When I reflected on my life, I wasn't too pleased with myself. I was having a lot of nightmares and cold sweats."

When a government-sponsored program offered Brendan a place in a white high school in the suburbs of Boston, he took it. "To join some gangs, you have to kill someone. And if you leave, you will be murdered. My gang was a little different. People knew me, and knew that I was serious about my education. I always loved going to school. My OGs would always point me out and say, 'He's going to make it.' They wanted me to go to school and better myself.

"My mother always told me 'You're better than that' when we saw hoodlums on our street. I just stayed away from Boston as much as possible. After a while, it worked. I wasn't a part of Heath anymore."

During his final year of high school, Brendan's mother urged him to look into City Year. City Year brings together young people from diverse racial, ethnic, and socioeconomic backgrounds for a demanding year of full-time community service and leadership development. The organization's members include college graduates, high school graduates, and people without high school diplomas.

Alan Khazei and Michael Brown, roommates at Harvard Law School, founded City Year in 1988 as a fifty-person summer pilot program in Boston. Cited by President Clinton as the model for his national service legislation, City Year has expanded to include hundreds of core members in cities all over the country.

Brendan sent in his application and was called in to City Year for an interview. "I go down there, and these were the most happy-go-lucky people I'd ever seen. They were really excited about what they were doing, and they were happy to see me."

Brendan was struck by the diversity of City Year, some of which made him uncomfortable. "You would have ex-gangbangers working side by side with rich, white college kids. I remember thinking, I'm not going to work with any faggots."

City Year corps members participate in a wide variety of service activities. Typical projects might give corps members a chance to serve as teachers' aides in public schools, renovate low-income housing, or volunteer in homeless shelters. "I remember thinking, 'You know what, I have a chance to give back something positive. Maybe I won't have nightmares anymore,'" Brendan said.

In return for a year of hard work, corps members receive a stipend plus a scholarship award at the end of their service for use toward higher education or job training, and they have access to college and career counseling services.

In addition to weekly leadership and community-building workshops, City Year requires corps members who have not graduated from high school to take high school equivalency classes. If they keep up with the work, corps members can earn their GEDs.

"We had to sign a contract that explained what was expected of us in terms of attendance, punctuality, and behavior. If you don't stick to the contract, you're out of the program. I had to be smart, sharp, and prompt at all times."

Brendan thought City Year's expectations were reasonable. "In the contract, it said, 'Be here at 8:15 A.M.' I don't care if you have been abused all your life, you can make it here at 8:15.

"We worked every day, Monday through Friday, 8:15 A.M. to 6 P.M., from September to June. We began each morning with PT, physical training. After the half hour of calisthenics, we fanned out in teams of ten to different project sites around the city."

The city of Boston supplied corps members with free subway passes as a demonstration of support. "You would always see City Year kids on the T, Boston's subway. It was easy to spot us: bright red jackets, black City Year sweatshirts, khaki pants, and Timberland boots," he said.

Brendan knew the program was going to be hard for him to stick to, so he made himself a promise on the first day. "I told myself that whatever was to happen, as far as I was to go, or as low as I was to go, no matter how hard it got, I was not going to quit."

Somewhat unexpectedly, Brendan found himself in charge of teaching photography in an after-school program for kids who lived in a housing project near Cambridge. "My team leader said, 'Okay, who likes photography?' I raised my hand and said, 'I've taken a few pictures.' He said, 'Great. You're the new photography teacher.' Some City Year people taught me everything they knew, and I read some books to learn more."

To get kids to sign up for his class, Brendan did an outreach program in the neighborhood. "I went out and got the kids most people wouldn't even think of talking to. The ones drinking the forties and smoking the weed at thirteen by the basketball courts."

Brendan convinced eighteen kids to sign up for his class. "I gave them different assignments and told them they were not allowed to come back unless they'd done their homework. I told them, 'If you are going to take a picture of something, have a story to tell with it. And if you don't have a story, make one up.' That was my way of opening their minds. Then I would have them write up the story as a way of teaching them spelling and English."

In addition to the regular workday, Brendan also threw himself into extracurricular activities at City Year. His fellow corps members elected Brendan to lead the Corps Action Council, a liaison group between corps members and administrators at City Year. "I gave speeches at meetings and people liked them. I would speak about urban violence, drugs, gangs, AIDS [Brendan's father had recently died of AIDS], and interracial relationships. Things that had affected my life."

When some of Brendan's speeches brought hundreds of cheering and crying people to their feet, higher-ups at City Year started giving Brendan even greater responsibilities and opportunities. "Michael Brown, the cofounder, took me with him on a trip to meet with senators in Washington, D.C. I discussed my life history and experience with City Year in a meeting where we asked for more support for the program. I shook hands with President Clinton.

"Best of all, City Year was planning to open a new site in Chicago and I was chosen to be on the expansion team that moved there. They sent the Chicago expansion team on a training retreat. My bags were packed and I was all ready to move to a new city."

Brendan never made it to Chicago. "On the very last day of training, I was playing basketball with some corps members. One guy, an ex–crack addict from South Boston, started talking shit to me. Then all of a sudden he took a basketball and threw it at my head."

Brendan's assailant came at him swinging, and a fight broke out. "He found himself on the ground right quick with my foot going down his throat. Unfortunately Michael and Alan were right there watching. They yanked me from the expansion team."

Alan Khazei agreed to meet with Brendan to discuss the incident. "I wanted a second chance. I told him, 'Dude, if someone came at you swinging, I'm sure you would defend yourself.' He said, 'No, I'd get punched in the face.' I said, 'Alan, as far as I'm concerned, if you came at me swinging, I'd knock you out, too. I don't know too many people who don't defend themselves and their family.'

"I knew that I was not God's gift to City Year, but I had really tried my best. That was the closest I came to quitting City Year, when Alan Khazei told me he would have taken those punches. I had done outreach programs at high schools for City Year and preached about City Year's diversity, open-mindedness, and commitment to giving people a second chance. I felt betrayed. Here's my top guy basically telling me 'Fuck you.' I almost felt like getting up and punching him to see what he really would have done."

Brendan decided to stick to his original promise and finished out his time with City Year. The mother of a fellow corps member had heard about Brendan and offered to help him get into college. "She said, 'Meet with me, and if you impress me, I will write a letter of recommendation on your behalf.' With her help, I got in," he said.

Brendan was accepted at Johnson C. Smith University in Charlotte, North Carolina. "I had never heard of the school, had never been down to the South, didn't know anything about Charlotte, and was very skeptical about going," he said.

Successfully completing City Year entitled Brendan to $5,000, money that helped convince him to give college a try. Going from the diversity of City Year to an all-black college was difficult. "There was some hatred toward whites on campus that was hard for me to deal with." Having a white mother and a black father sometimes made life complicated for Brendan. "Being a mulatto was hard. Lots of Oreo cookie jokes," he said.

Brendan's favorite class was one where he read *Jonathan Livingston Seagull* by Richard Bach. The book is about a seagull whose love for flying isolates him from his fellow birds. "I told the people in the class that I felt like an outsider because I couldn't agree with what they were saying about white people.

When they said, 'All white people do this,' I said, 'You're wrong. My mother is white and she doesn't do that. My mother gave up her life to raise me and my brother.'"

Brendan plans to finish college and then pursue a master's degree in social work. "I want to spend my life reaching back, helping other people in situations like mine to get out.

"There needs to be a change. There are 27,000 golf courses in America, and we still have people living in the streets who can't feed themselves."

Would he recommend City Year to other people? "City Year has problems just like any other organization. They're not perfect, but they're trying. Is City Year right for you? I don't know you. You better look into it yourself."

Brendan said the most important thing he learned was to accept people for who they are. "I met the first gay person I'd ever respected. It opened my mind to the fact that gays are just like everyone else. They should not be treated like faggots, because they're not faggots. That's like calling a black person a nigger. They're not niggers; they're human beings."

For more information . . .

www.cityyear.org—Get plugged in to the City Year program in one of the (at last count) seventeen cities in which it operates a program. You can read about its history, member profiles, and the activities in which City Year is currently engaged.

A City Year: On the Streets and in the Neighborhoods with Twelve Young Community Service Volunteers, by Suzanne Goldsmith. Transaction Publishers, 1997. A personal telling of a former City Year participant's experiences with the youth-service program.

Susan Steele
UNIVERSITY OF VERMONT
Went to Colorado to teach disabled kids to ski

Susan Steele knew it was possible to take time off after finishing high school in Woodstock, Vermont. She just wasn't sure it was desirable.

"In this town, there are very few opportunities. If you are my age and you are not in college, and you don't have some sort of career, you're basically going to be stuck in a five-dollar-an-hour, dead-end job. I didn't want that, so I went ahead and enrolled at the University of Vermont."

Susan adjusted to college-level academics more easily than she had expected, in part because she was not required to study the subjects that had plagued her in high school. "I have some learning disabilities, and they hit me hardest in math and languages—subjects that you just can't avoid in high school. I had to work very hard, and it was very stressful for me. I thought I would never make it in college, that I would fail out in my first year."

But it was financial reality, encountered at the end of her sophomore year, that caused Susan to think seriously about taking time off. "A lot of it came down to money. My brother had just finished school, which meant that I got less financial aid. Because my parents were no longer paying his tuition, the financial-aid officer at UVM calculated that more of their income should now be available to pay UVM's tuition. My parents knew I was thinking about taking a year off, and they really believed it would be good for me."

Susan began to look around for things to do. "I was looking for an internship. I didn't have to make any money; I just couldn't spend any. I decided that what I truly wanted was to get involved with an environmental center that emphasized science more than just outdoor skills."

After compiling a long list of centers that interested her, Susan began making phone calls. "I didn't know about any of these places or what they were looking for. Some of them were really prestigious, and many of them wanted you to be a graduate student."

Susan found a job at Hobart Outdoor Center in Fairlee, Vermont. She began work there after spending the summer as a camp counselor.

"Hobart was such an amazing experience. It is set up for groups of schoolchildren that come for a few days at a time. Classes come, and the teachers break them up into groups of ten or twelve. Usually the teachers put together kids who don't necessarily get along. So when they come to us, we set up challenges for them in an outdoor environment that they have to overcome as a group. Trust falls, a ropes course, teamwork exercises—things like that.

"Afterward, we try to talk about it, what went right, how they felt in a particular role. If a kid is always the leader in the group, we try to get him to be a follower and get the follower to be the leader, just to get kids to experiment and think about how they treat one another.

"I think the best thing about the program was that all the staff that came in that year was new, and everyone was so excited to learn. I felt like I took in so much in so little time. It has given me the strength to deal interpersonally, which was a great experience to bring with me to what followed after that."

Susan's job at Hobart was only a two-month stint, and midway through her time there she had not found another job. At that point, she started looking back through her notes, and a place called the Breckenridge Outdoor Education Center caught her eye.

"When I first looked at the information, I had no idea that a large part of what they did there was teach disabled people to ski. I'd never worked with kids with disabilities before, and that really intimidated me. How would I react in a situation like that?

"One of the big reasons I decided to go was that they seemed so nice initially. They sent me information right away, when I hadn't heard from all these other places at all. And when I called from Hobart to find out more, the woman I talked to was so nice. Then, after I knew I was going, I kept running into people who had done this internship. Everyone said, 'Definitely go; it will be the greatest experience of your life.'"

When Susan first interviewed for the Breckenridge internship over the phone, the staff there led her to expect the worst. "I was expecting six months of hell," she recalled. "My boss kept insisting what a tough job it was, telling me how cold it was and that we lived in this cabin three miles from the nearest shower.

"I was actually a little disappointed when I got there and discovered that there was a town between my cabin and my shower and that the shower was at a health club. I was expecting to have to dig outhouses."

Susan lived in a cabin with all the other volunteers, who were mostly in their twenties and early thirties. The cabin was heated with wood, and the volunteers shared in the cooking duties.

When Susan arrived, she found that she was going to be living with Mandy, a woman about her age from the University of Michigan. "I was out skiing the day Mandy moved in. When I came back, all her stuff was there, her mountain bike, and her helmet. I just had this feeling that we were really similar people."

Susan quickly discovered that for all they had in common, she and Mandy had important differences as well. "I was not expecting her to have only one leg. When she first walked in, I kind of gulped. Wow, was

I surprised. At first I wasn't sure how to treat her. I didn't know when or whether to ask her if she needed help, because I didn't want to offend her.

"But then I realized, well, how am I going to know if I don't ask? And so I would ask and take her word for it when she said, 'No, I don't want any help carrying this.' A lot of people in her life ask her if she needs help, and just asking doesn't make her angry. It's when they don't take her word for it when she says no that sets her off."

Breckenridge was like Hobart in that it also had an outdoor education/ team-building course, but most Breckenridge interns spend at least 80 percent of their time on the slopes. Philosophically, the two places were very different.

"I'm the kind of person who is a nurturer, and my past work experiences really drew on those skills," Susan said. "The philosophy at Breckenridge is more to just let loose and have fun. There's definitely not any pity involved, no consoling. They're really hard on their participants, in a good way. It's a real challenge."

At Breckenridge, Susan explained, the mountain was the great equalizer. "Everybody on skis is disabled, because everyone is a fool when they have these long fiberglass things on. Skiing for people who can't walk can be the most liberating, enlightening thing, because for a change they aren't fighting gravity. Gravity is finally helping them, and it's the one time they can really go fast," Susan said.

Susan was constantly learning more about what it was like to be physically disabled. "There was a blind woman who had done some teaching with us, and she had a 'disability dinner'—where everyone was assigned a different disability. I was blind, some people didn't have limbs, and we had to work together to get the meal cooked.

"We ended up re-creating the disability dinner when a lot of our groups came up. It was great, because it opens up all this discussion about how you treat each other during the dinner, which leads directly into discussions of how people are treated, or want to be treated."

Groups of skiers came from all over the country, and each person presented unique challenges. "Every lesson was different, because every disability is different," Susan said. "You just have to always be prepared to come up with a way to solve a problem. Whether it's a four-runner for a person in a wheelchair or dealing with special equipment for limb losses or acting as a guide for a blind skier, you have to be able to look at a situation and say, 'Okay, this is not working. How am I going to fix it?'"

In addition to room and board, Susan received a fifty-dollar monthly stipend, which she said was plenty. "There really wasn't a lot of stress. People took good care of us in town, invited us over for meals and things, because they thought we were doing such good work. And a lot of times the older students would want to take us out to bars, and to disco night."

Susan's time at Breckenridge was finite, since she knew she was going to work at a camp for the summer. "I used to dread going back to school," she said. "I would go to Boulder sometimes and look at the university there and get the willies. My job was so much more fun. I guess what I enjoyed most was coming home at night after teaching and just having that be my time and not having to stress about all this work."

When she returned to school, Susan found she had changed in unexpected ways. "I had always been a pretty quiet person, but in Colorado I went out more than I had ever done in my entire life," she said. "When I got back to school, I was definitely more social, meeting more people."

She also got herself out of the dorms. "I was living in an apartment with one of my friends from freshman year and two other women. I think that made all the difference in the world.

"The hardest part about coming back was the fact that the amount I learned during my time off, you can't even compare it to the type of things you learn in school," she said. "In some ways, I felt like I was just waiting out the rest of my time here."

Susan said that this problem was especially apparent in an English class she took her first semester back at UVM. "Whenever I went to work on my English, it was always to work on this one essay I was writing about Mandy," she said. "I really wanted to make that one right. I let all my other work in the class slack, and I ended up handing in an incomplete portfolio.

"I didn't know how my grade would reflect that, and you know what? It doesn't really matter. I think I did what was important, and that's the most significant thing. That semester was where I processed my experience and my relationship with Mandy, what it was, why it was important, and what I gained from being with her and being out there.

"My geography class that semester, and my geology class, sure, they were great. But will I ever use that information again? Probably not, no. I think that's part of what was so important about my year away. I will always use the things I learned."

For more information . . .

www.boec.org—Learn how to get involved with the Adaptive Skiing Program with the Breckenridge Outdoor Education Center.

Part 3

Study

Ben Coolik

UNIVERSITY OF GEORGIA

Spent a year in Israel in a program specifically for young people taking a year off before college

---

Ben Coolik never doubted that he would spend a year in Israel between high school and college. His only problem was convincing everyone else.

Ben went to a private school in Columbus, Georgia, for thirteen years. "It was predominately white and Christian. Growing up, I participated in Young Judaea, a national youth movement that seeks to promote Israel. I went to camps and weekend programs, which was great for me, because I got to hang out with all these other Jewish kids.

"Young Judaea has a yearlong course in Israel for about 150 people who have just graduated from high school. They're really big on their program, so Year Course is hammered into your head as you're growing up. By freshman year of high school, I knew I was going to do it," he said.

Ben's high school promoted a more traditional route. "Everyone was on the college track. Their college matriculation rate is 100 percent, and their dropout rate is zero. They never mentioned time off. I don't think anyone had ever even thought of it.

"At first, I don't think they were too excited about me going. The biggest question was, how can we fix this where we have him graduating and going to college so we don't lose our 100 percent rate in the national rankings? The alumni magazine came out when we graduated in the spring of 1993, and next to my name they wrote 'University of Georgia, Fall of 1994.' Not a word about me going to Israel," he recalled.

Ben's father was also skeptical, and it took an all-out lobbying effort to turn him around. "My dad said 'No' when I was a freshman, 'No' when I was a sophomore. Then, when I was a junior, he said, 'We'll see.' I started talking to people in the Young Judaea office to get them to talk to him about it, tell him success stories. I just worked him and worked him.

"His biggest problem? Whether I would ever come back. That I would want to stay forever or join the Israeli Army or something. There was also the war and the propaganda on TV. He thought of Israel as some big desert battlefield."

This was before the violence in the region had escalated to the levels it has recently reached, and Ben's father eventually decided that Ben should go after all. "When he finally broke down, it wasn't even a breakdown, it was a complete change in position," Ben recalled. "He said, 'Ben, you are going to Israel. I have talked to so many people who told me what a great thing it is in so many ways that I wouldn't want you to do anything else at this point."

Ben's father also wanted him to go to college, preferably at his alma mater, the University of Georgia. Ben spent the summer after high school taking classes at the Columbus branch of the state university system so that he could still graduate from college four years after he finished high school. Right after Labor Day, though, he packed his bags and drove to the Columbus airport.

"My dad was crying at the airport, and I felt bad, but it didn't really hit me until I got to Atlanta to change planes to fly to Kennedy in New York. Then I was flooded with all these emotions.

"I looked around the plane, realizing that I was going to be with strangers for an entire year, and I broke down in tears. The old lady sitting next to me asked me what was wrong, and I told her that I was leaving home to spend a year in Israel. Well, that's where she was going! So she starts telling me all these great things about how wonderful Israel is, how pretty the girls are. She just totally made me happy," he recalled.

When Ben arrived in New York, he met up with his group, the first step of the Year Course. His year was divided into different segments designed to give students as broad an exposure to Israeli life as possible.

Ben's group was a cross section of standard teenage stereotypes: "There was Ira from Texas, and all he talked about was hunting and his truck. There were a couple of Deadheads with goatees and Afros. There were girls from New York who thought they were cool because they listened to Phish. There was one really rich guy from Beverly Hills. Then there was this guy from Miami who had all these crazy outfits and was really into bodybuilding."

After a brief orientation session in the airport, two counselors herded them onto their flight. "When we first got there, they had us all think for a few minutes about why we were there, just to get our minds set for the year. At that age, you're basically the sum of everything you've been taught. I wanted to find out more about what kind of person *I* was and what kind of personal goals *I* wanted to set for myself."

Like all Year Course groups, Ben's group started their year in Jerusalem with a weeklong orientation. The group then headed north to Ma'alot, about twenty miles from the Lebanese border, where they spent ten weeks working.

Israeli development towns were originally built to help absorb new immigrants quickly. New arrivals could get housing easily, learn Hebrew, and receive instruction on finding employment and a permanent place to live. As Israel has grown, however, the area around the immigrant absorption center in Ma'alot has grown as well, and today it is a full-fledged town in its own right.

Ben's group lived in a small apartment in the absorption center and performed manual labor there in exchange for rent. Each student also had a community project, and Ben chose to volunteer in the local high school.

"I taught conversational English to eleventh and twelfth graders. We painted a bomb shelter in the high school and turned it into a classroom. The teachers would bring their students down, and they would ask us all sorts of questions about America."

Ben made friends with several of his students and spent weekends with them in their homes and in the local bar. "It was this small wooden place, and the bartender let us run a tab because we were all so broke. Ira would bring in Garth Brooks [albums], and we would just listen to music and hang out."

For the first few weeks Ben's group also spent three hours a day in an intensive Hebrew language class. "The language was a big obstacle in Ma'alot. It's not necessary to know the language in other parts of the country, but there they wanted us to get over it quickly," he said.

After a weeklong hike in December, Ben's group spent three weeks on an Israeli Army base. "We had to wake up at five-thirty, put on fatigues, do calisthenics, and eat in the mess hall. Some Israelis think it's bullshit, that we're just out there playing toy soldier while they're fighting to keep the country alive. But for us it was cool to see what life was like for kids our age who have to be in the army.

"We took it pretty seriously. They had this one tank storage room that they needed to tear down to make the tank fields bigger, so we were in there moving fifty-pound bales of barbed wire out," he said.

In January, Ben's group returned to Jerusalem for the academic portion of the program, which included more intensive Hebrew instruction, classes on Zionism and geography, and electives. Classes were graded, but a pass/fail option was available, and many students were able to obtain college credit for the courses when they returned to the States.

Ben and his group then traveled to the Golan Mountains in northeastern Israel to spend time on a *moshav. Moshavim* are planned communities where families farm their own land (as opposed to *kibbutzim,* where the land is communally owned) and meet collectively to address matters that affect everyone.

"A lot of people take advantage of that time to live with a family that doesn't speak English, so they can really work on their Hebrew. But part of the point also is to learn what it is like living with an Israeli family.

"I worked in the flower fields on my hands and knees for six hours every day. I also worked in the palmetto fields, picking off the rotten ones and setting rat poison. I got up really early, and it just felt so good. After the work was done, we'd pick oranges and lemons and grapefruits off the trees and make these amazing juices," he said.

Ben noted that the sense of community on a *moshav* is incredibly strong. "I worked with the turkeys some, and they all got very sick while I was there. It was cool to watch everyone come together to figure out what was wrong and then to pitch in for vaccinations."

Most Young Judaea groups do a two-month stint on a *kibbutz.* Ben's did not, but he said it's possible to arrange for *kibbutz* stays of varying length.

Year Course participants also spend several weeks as volunteers in a profession of their choice. Ben decided to work in a theater in Jerusalem. "The options are endless, and Young Judaea will help you find something that interests you. I had done a lot of theater as a child, and I wanted to do some technical work. I started calling around, and one place said that it might have an opening. Their tech person had just quit, so I kept calling and calling, and they finally gave me a job because I was so persistent.

"They had a real simple light board, and I repatched it. I worked hard at it, and they appreciated the fact that I was putting so much effort into something that I wasn't getting paid for. I did lights for the Friday-night jazz jam, where they had Irish, Balkan, and flamenco music, and for a two-act play, too.

"I would work from six until midnight. Then I would clean up, go out until four in the morning, then sleep until four the next day. That was my lifestyle for six weeks. It was a really cool time.

"I've heard people say that it is hard to make it in Israel, but if you're American and you have some kind of skill or talent, it's so easy. They would have hired me for a paying job if I had been able to stay."

After a tearful weekend of good-byes, Ben returned home to reflect a bit before starting school in the fall. "Israel was very much a cultural awakening for me. In America, we use religion as a basis of how Jewish we are. But when you're in Israel, it's the Jewish state, so you don't really have to prove your religiousness.

"I was totally alone in a strange country. Having to worry about yourself—that's a tremendous responsibility, if you think about it. But that's the great thing about the program. You learn to handle that without getting bogged down by it," he added.

Ben maintained a perfect 4.0 during his first two quarters as a finance major at UGA. "Everybody called me 'Mr. Dad' because they thought I was so responsible about everything. But during the first quarter my dad told me that I was studying too much. I mean, that was my *father* talking."

Ben's experiences in the theater left an indelible mark on him as well. While he wanted to study theater in college, his father convinced him to concentrate on finance and business, since even a career in the arts would require good business sense. His head for numbers came in handy after college; he spent time working the cash register and the tables at casinos run by a father of a friend of his. He also continued to satisfy his wanderlust, taking long hiking trips and traveling abroad.

Ben graduated from the University of Georgia in 1998 with a degree in business, but he's since returned and is currently studying toward a master's degree in theater lighting design. Though his undergraduate courses didn't give him the necessary qualifications for the program, his experience in Israel working in the theater convinced the professors running the program to take a chance on him.

While Ben still believes that going to Israel is one of the best things he's ever done, he knows how much courage it would take for parents to send their kids there right now. Still, he believes that going to Israel now is somewhat akin to joining the Peace Corps. "There's strife, corruption, violence," he said. "But despite such adverse conditions, people are there living their lives the best way that they can, and compassionate folks are visiting there to offer help in whatever way they can. What would happen if all the parents in the world were successful in persuading their children not to visit such places? Their fear for the safety of their children would snuff out the very heart of humanitarianism.

"There are babies being born there as we speak, kids going to elementary school, high schoolers going to malls and discotheques, mothers and fathers enjoying careers and raising families. Life there hasn't stopped because of the violence. In fact, it's because of the threat of violence that the people of the region have learned how valuable life really is.

"The tragedy of September 11 shows us that even here in the States we are subject to terrorist violence. And I would guess that America has a higher crime rate than Israel in terms of other forms of violence: assault, rape, and kidnapping. And despite that, we feel safer and more secure here. Why is that? It is my belief that the only difference is the perspective you take on it."

For more information . . .

www.youngjudaea.org—Official website of the Young Judaea program.

www.israelprogramscenter.org—"A one-stop location providing information on Israel travel and study programs." Offers information on scholarship programs, educational materials, referrals to other agencies, and a list of seminars.

www.livnot.org.il—Website of Livnot U'Lehibanot, a work-study program for twenty-one- to thirty-year-olds interested in exploring their cultural and religious identities while in Israel.

www.kibbutzprogramcenter.org—The Kibbutz Program Center provides information about volunteer opportunities to work and live on *kibbutzim* in Israel, including details about stipends, insurance, the variety of *kibbutzim*, and locations in Israel.

Celia Quezada
WILLIAMS COLLEGE
Spent a year in Belgium on a Rotary Club scholarship

In the early 1960s, Celia Quezada's father left Mexico to work in the United States through the Bracero Program, an agreement between the U.S. and Mexico that brought Mexican guest workers into the U.S. for seasonal agricultural labor. "My father drove a tractor, and my mother did jobs like hoeing weeds during the lettuce season, bunching onions, and packing tomatoes. When I was younger, I sometimes worked with my mom in the fields," she said.

Growing up, Celia felt caught between two cultures. The high cost of living in the United States during the months when her parents had no work would force her family to return temporarily to Mexico from Gonzales, California. "Every year during the rainy season, we would migrate back to Mexico. Even though our home was in the States, Mexico lived within me. Little kids used to hate me when I went back; they called me the *gringa*."

Just before beginning high school, Celia experienced what she views as her biggest break. "In eighth grade I didn't know universities existed. I just knew that after high school I had to find a job somehow. I thought that maybe I could be a secretary for some lawyer," she said.

That summer, Celia went to a special seminar at the University of California at Santa Cruz known as the *Yo Puedo* program. "*Yo Puedo* is Spanish for 'I Can,' and it was part of a program conducted by the state of California for the children of migrant farm workers. "It totally enlightened me. They taught me about financial aid and universities. They said I didn't have to stick to California. They made me believe that I could do it," she recalled.

"I went for all of it. In high school, I stuck my nose in everything. I wanted to change the world; I was Miss Gung-ho." Celia had to juggle her many extracurricular activities with responsibilities at home. "I'd get home at six, then I had to clean the house and cook, because if your mom is working, someone has to do it. You can't make her do everything. I wouldn't start studying until nine and then I'd go to bed around 2 A.M."

Celia was president of her school's student body. She felt that the majority of the students didn't care about the school's Spanish-speaking population. "Every time I took the microphone in front of people, I would translate. I noticed that every time we chose the staff member of the month, it was a teacher. I asked, 'What about the cafeteria workers, the bus drivers, the custodians? If they weren't here, who would be cleaning your toilets? It would be a pigsty.' So we acknowledged them. It's a question of treating people like people."

She was accepted at Williams College, the first person in her family to continue with education after high school. Celia's parents fully supported her college plans, but they became apprehensive when she contemplated postponing her studies to spend a year in Europe with the Rotary Club's exchange program.

Celia made it to the final round in Rotary's application process and was then required to bring her parents in for an interview. "They asked my parents the question I'll never forget," Celia recalled. "'Do you realize you will not see your daughter for one entire year?'" Celia saw her parents' eyes begin to get teary. It seemed for a moment that they might not be willing to let her go. "Whatever's best for my daughter," Celia's parents declared. "Whatever she decides."

Celia won a scholarship from Rotary, but instead of offering her one of the three countries she had listed on a preference questionnaire, they proposed to send her to Belgium. "I didn't even know Belgium existed,"

Celia said. "People would ask me, 'Haven't you heard of Belgian waffles? And Brussels sprouts?'"

After she graduated from high school, Celia went through some last-minute jitters. "I did not want to go," she explained. "What the hell was I going to do in Europe? I always thought that was for snobs."

Celia's anxieties worsened when her host family greeted her at the airport in Brussels. "They had a Jaguar, so immediately I was intimidated. Then I saw that all the taxis were Mercedes Benzes or Volvos and that some of the highway patrolmen drove Porsches. 'This,' I thought to myself, 'is a wealthy country.'"

Celia had difficulty with her first host family, which added to the challenges of adjusting to life in a foreign country. "They would always speak English to me, so I couldn't learn Flemish," she said. "And the little girl was always shoving a dictionary at me and saying, 'Learn it! Learn it!' Then, to top it off, my host mother was reading my diary. So I wrote in my diary, 'I know she reads my diary, and she's stupid for doing that.'"

Celia convinced Rotary to find her another family. She advises those who feel trapped in difficult situations to stick up for themselves. "Don't be afraid to say that something is making you uncomfortable or unhappy," she said. "If you're on a program and get assigned to a family that is not working out for you, ask to be switched if you're sure you have given it a fair chance."

Celia's second family turned out to be literally a second family to her. Her new host father announced that he didn't speak English very well and that Celia was going to have to learn Flemish. "That's why you're here," he told Celia. "I started speaking Flemish, and I became really close to the family. They ended up buying me a plane ticket so that I could go back and visit them a year later," she said.

Rotary arranged for Celia to enroll as a student at a local school. "It was a drag sometimes, not being able to understand what was going on in school. I ended up going to a fifth-grade French class. Sitting in the middle of all these kids, I thought to myself, 'At least I'm learning something.' I also went to Flemish night classes."

"I was so used to doing the right thing at home, but in Belgium I didn't know what the right thing was. The trick for me was being open-minded. You have to accept the culture the way it is."

Celia wanted to see some more of Europe while she was there. Sometimes she was able to tag along with her host family for free. She also discovered a creative way to raise her own travel funds. "I cooked a huge Mexican meal for all the Rotary members. They paid me for everything I needed for the meal; they paid for my trip and gave me a few hundred dollars [for] spending money," she said. Celia ultimately was able to visit Paris, London, Prague, and Vienna.

After her Rotary year was over, Celia returned home to California before starting Williams College.

"Taking time off was one of the most important things that ever happened to me," she said. "It took courage to stick it out and not give up. My parents instilled in me a drive to always do more, to not hang around in this measly little town of Gonzales. So even though I got to the point with my first host family where I felt like jumping out of my second-floor window, at least to break my leg so I could be sent home, I knew that coming home early would be letting everyone down. Once I made up my mind to stay and make the best of it, I found myself doing things that I would never have seen myself doing here. I became more independent. I think it really helped me grow.

"Taking time off also made me respect my parents even more than I did before. For all they went through, for all they struggled for. All I had ever really known was Gonzales, this small little town. It was great to see what it is like out there in the world. A lot of students who go straight to college don't even know what the heck the real world is. They've always been supported by Mommy and Daddy, who give them money and a pat on the back. 'Oh, here, honey, I found you a job.' Because everything has been given to them on a silver platter, they have no idea how the real world works.

"I was very lucky because my parents emphasized education as a way to get ahead. My parents always tell me, 'Whatever is best for you, as long as you don't end up in the fields.'"

For more information . . .

See General Resources, Study, Study Abroad, page 243.

Eric Van Dusen
UNIVERSITY OF CALIFORNIA AT BERKELEY
Enrolled in a university in Argentina and traveled
overland back to the United States

Pick any point on a map, and Eric Van Dusen will tell you how to get there. Having journeyed through Central and South America, Eric believes that in life, as in traveling, "there is always a bus to the next town."

Eric's chance to take time off materialized in a roundabout way. "I skipped the first grade, and family folklore maintained that my preciousness entitled me to take a sabbatical from school sometime in the future," he explained. "Most important, my dad was a believer in this family folklore. And he was the person in the family who made you go to school when you were sick. So if he thought it was okay, so did everyone else."

"I went to Marblehead High School in Massachusetts, and during my senior year everyone was asking me about colleges. 'Where are you going to school, Eric? Where? Where?'"

Although he was rejected by most of the colleges he applied to, Eric did manage to get into the University of California at Berkeley, but for the spring semester, not for the fall.

Eric's initial disappointment faded as he started planning his time off. "In retrospect, I think it was really good that I didn't get into some prestigious New England school. The change of perspective by coming out here to California and escaping Marblehead was huge."

After graduating from high school in June, Eric lived at home and worked at the local boatyard until late October. "I was pumping gas and trying to save up money so I could do something. Not being in school during the month of September was enlightening for me. I had been conditioned every year of my life to believe that summer ended on Labor Day. What a hoax. There I was, living at home and working at the local boatyard. I also got a painting job. It was incredible. September was just as nice as August. Every single person I knew was in school, and I was so psyched that I was free," he said.

Living at home, however, was not always easy for Eric. "I felt like a chump to be living at home, because I wasn't in high school anymore. Everyone was calling me from college with crazy stories, and I was just sitting at home, not doing anything. Time off gave me a brief glimpse of existential angst: 'Well, what do I do if I'm not in high school and I'm not in college? What is the meaning of life?'"

At the end of October, Eric left Marblehead for Guatemala. He stayed there through December and then returned to the United States to start his first semester at Berkeley in January.

Eric gives his mother partial credit for his decision to go to Guatemala. "Our coffee table was stacked thick and sagging in the middle with publications of the East Coast liberal establishment. It was a heavy Reagan-era period, the Contras, El Salvador. I was reading a lot about current events. My mom said, 'Why don't you talk to your aunt and uncle? They just came back from a great trip to Guatemala.'"

With the endorsement of his aunt and uncle, Eric convinced his parents to pay $600 for six weeks of language study and living with a family. "That way," said Eric, "my parents could know that I was going to study." He paid for his airfare and travel expenses.

Eric was slightly overwhelmed when he first arrived in the country. "I walked around in Guatemala City, which is this super-hellish Third World city full of really poor people. I was walking around by myself, seventeen years old, with a crew cut. I was thinking, 'This is so crazy. What am I doing here?' I had no idea what it would be like. No clue.

"The big Guatemalan oppression was in the early eighties, when they grabbed people from their homes and shot them randomly in the streets every night. By the time I was there in 1987, everything was comparatively mellow."

Eric joined what he calls the *gringo* influx of people who attend language school in Guatemala. He lived with an Indian family and received six hours of one-on-one language instruction each day during the week.

"Every weekend, I was doing something. It was so easy to meet people. I was in Antigua, a city in Guatemala where a lot of people are sent to learn Spanish by their NGO, their nongovernmental organization. Being seventeen was no problem; everyone thought I was twenty-five. There was always somebody young and hip and ready to go somewhere, or somebody who knew where to go and could tell me. They knew which bus to take and how to get to the rad waterfall in the jungle.

"Guatemala is such an amazing country to travel in. Packed into an area the size of Virginia, you have jungles, the Pacific Ocean, the Caribbean Sea, high mountains, the indigenous culture of the Indians—all within two hours of one another."

Eric noticed many travelers whose imaginations were restricted by the guidebooks they were using. "There's this thing about people backpacking and traveling with books, like the Lonely Planet guides. They're useful, and I've done a lot of traveling like that. But if you use that book to get to the rad waterfall in the jungle, there will be fifteen other people there when you arrive.

"It's so much more empowering when you can go do it on your own. Show up in a town and ask, 'Where can we stay?' And you get led around in circles until you find a place. Then you can ask, 'Where can we eat?' And the town may be so small that there's only one place. So you go there."

Immersing himself in one-on-one Spanish instruction proved to be challenging for Eric. "Sitting down with someone one-on-one for six hours a day was painful sometimes, but that's the way to learn. My learning curve was so steep. You just have to be patient, and realize that it is unnatural to talk to someone six hours a day for five days in a row. Sometimes my instructor would look at me and say, 'You talk now.'

"Guatemala is a very poor country. Per capita income is much less than in the United States. Room and board, which includes three meals a day, five days a week, costs twenty to thirty dollars a week. You can live with an Indian family of five people in a one-room home. And they have one extra bed where three of the kids were going to sleep. Now they're all going to sleep in the bed with the two parents and the other two kids, so that you can sleep in that bed. Other schools can hook you up with nicer accommodations, but then you may not have the same contact with the indigenous community."

Eric left Guatemala in December and came home to get ready for college. He said he was a bit confused about what to expect at Berkeley. He took a class in Latin American history during his first semester. "I totally lived for and loved that class. We studied Argentina and Chile. I also took a class on economic development. The professor made me realize that studying development and the Third World was something you could do in life. I decided to visit the countries I had been studying."

At first, Eric hoped to find a traditional study abroad program such as Education Abroad Programs at Berkeley. "But to do EAP, you have to have taken two years of Spanish classes at Berkeley. And I'm not good at doing little homework assignments, like writing down everything with the right accent mark over and over again. Also, it's really hard to figure out from here what is up in other countries. What's the place to be? What's the good school?

"I decided to buy a one-way ticket to go from California to Chile. School doesn't start down there until March, so I thought I could figure out how to enroll and take classes once I arrived."

Eric discovered that there are many different ways to travel. "Sometimes in Chile I was just into the drug of traveling, into being constantly moving. I had to adjust to that more voyeuristic pace. When you see the fat American tourist pointing his video camera at the little Indian girl in the village, it's a lot weirder than seeing him point it at a cathedral in the middle of the city.

"You can be totally self-sufficient with a backpack, tent, and stove. I usually tried to find a home to stay in, and there were a lot of bed-and-breakfast-style places. You can just ask, 'Where can I stay? Do you know somebody with a room?' That way, you get to actually meet real people. You can sit in their living room and look at their pictures. They may tell you stories about their cousin living in Houston: 'Don't you know Houston? Do you know my cousin?'

"So much of people trying to learn Spanish results in a tourist saying, 'How much is this? Can I buy that?' or 'Where's the bus?' But to be able to have a conversation means being able to hear their story.

"Crime wasn't so bad in Chile. Peru was where you hear the hairy stories. People there may go at your backpack with a machete, and ten little kids will dive on your stuff while it spills out before you have a chance to grab it."

Border crossings were another occasion for heads-up behavior. Though Eric was seldom searched himself, he experienced firsthand the high drama of covert crossings from one country into another. "I was on a crowded bus driving across the border between Chile and Bolivia. The security guy came on and I was all worried about him coming to search me because I'm a *gringo* with long hair. And then I realized there was a forty-year-old fat *señora* across from me, smuggling 10,000 Snickers candy bars from the duty-free port in Chile into Bolivia. She pretended to be asleep, and when the security guy asked her what was in the bags, she said, '*Ropa, ropa*. Clothes. Leave me alone.'"

After spending January, February, and part of March traveling in Chile and Bolivia, Eric went to Argentina. "The first day I got there, I said, 'Here I am, ta-da! I'm going to register for my classes.' The janitor was locking up the door, and he told me, 'Oh, sorry. Everyone is on strike.'

"So I head downtown, and there is a huge protest going on in the central plaza. Drums, flags, chants, and all these labor movements—including the teachers' union. I was so psyched to see a protest where labor was a real force."

School finally started two weeks later, and Eric signed up for a full load of courses. He was initially living with other Americans in a "random fucked-up hotel that I read about in a tourist guide," which wasn't helping his Spanish. "So I posted some signs that said, 'I am an American student looking for a place to share, please leave your phone number.' And people left their numbers. I ended up living with a great Argentinean guy in his twenties. I hooked up with his friends, and we would stay up late to drink, play chess, and sit around listening to tango."

Eric's style of studying abroad proved to be much cheaper than a regular program would have been. "It was so cheap because I was going to the state school and living in an apartment. It was $600 the first semester at school, and through Berkeley's EAP program it cost $3,000. And if you're willing to jump through a lot of paperwork hoops, you can get credit on your transcript," he said.

Eric strove for a more authentic experience than many people on exchange programs achieve. "The greatest thing for me was that I could just fit in and be a student. I didn't open my mouth in class for the first month. I would just go and sit there and take notes. And nobody noticed.

"I met a bunch of Americans taking classes at another university with a formal study abroad program. They were having a good time, but educationally it was a total joke. And everything was facilitated for them: 'Let's go to the meeting together. Let's have the little luncheon for all the exchange students.' Those people were still on the tour bus.

"For me to show up in Argentina, find an Argentinean to live with, go to the UBA [the University of Buenos Aires], walk in, figure out which class I wantcd to go to by reading the schedule, go and sit in on a class, buy the reading from the school store, and go through the paces of a student without anyone telling me what to do—all that gave me a sense of empowerment."

After spending a semester at the UBA, Eric capped off his trip with a 6,000-mile, thirty-day overland excursion, passing through fifteen countries on his way home from Buenos Aires to Berkeley.

"I had $650, which was the cost of a one-way plane ticket home. I figured I could travel home in twelve hours with a freaky microwave meal and a beer. Or I could have a whole month of adventures," he said.

"You can always get a bus to the next town, and you can always get a visa at the border. I was taking buses and trains, mostly buses, and hitchhiking."

Traversing the Darien Gap, which separates Colombia from Panama, was the trickiest part of Eric's journey home. "Panama was wild. From Colombia to Panama I went in a motorboat, bouncing off the Caribbean waves at six in the morning. We hit this tiny village, a random outpost of civilization. All mangoes, coconuts, and fish. Impenetrable jungle. And there were no roads.

"A Panamanian border patrolman searched me, and when he realized I was American, he walked inside and yelled, 'Hey, come out here, I've got an American for you.' Two marines came out who were stationed in Panama following the U.S. invasion.

"One of them says to me, 'Oh, you're one of those longhaired hippie types trying to save Central America and make it safe for the Commies.' A total asshole trying to pick a fight with me. 'No, sir,' I said. 'I'm just on my way home from the university.'

"I went to the only place around where you could eat lunch and drink a beer. While I was there, this huge military helicopter lands, and out steps the colonel. He is walking down the main street and looks over at me. And there I am, sitting in my chair drinking a beer. I have on a T-shirt with Edvard Munch's painting *The Scream,* of a guy with no ears standing on a bridge and filling the whole canvas with his anguished howl. My T-shirt was captioned 'President Quayle.'

"'Who's that?' asks the colonel.

"'Uh, I don't know, sir. He's a visiting traveling student, sir.'

"So the colonel comes over to say hello and ask me if I'm enjoying my stay. He's talking to me as if this situation is totally normal. So I ask him, 'Please, sir, might I have a ride across the Darien Gap with you? Please, can I go on the chopper? Because the only way for me to get out of here is to hike through the jungle for a week.'

"'Not with that shirt you won't,' the colonel told me.

"So I took the mail plane that comes through once a week. We flew over a huge coral archipelago, landing on these tiny islands. Water, airstrip, water—it's totally hairy. And there's a guy sitting in a hammock by the runway. Turns out he's the mailman. He gets up, saunters over. The pilot gives him two letters, and he gives him one letter, and we get back in the plane.

"We stopped at one settlement where Indians came up in huge dugout canoes, with big necklaces, totally dressed up, and put one of their guys on the plane next to me. He's never been on a plane before, so he's petrified. And we take off as they're canoeing away, waving up to us. Half an hour later, we were in Panama City.

"The way I made it across from South to Central America was not in any book at all. I just did it by going to the next town. There's always a way to go to the next town," Eric said.

"I definitely recommend taking time off. Get as far off the beaten track you can. For some people, going to Europe can be a truly amazing experience. For others, it's Eurail hell. 'Oh, and then we went to Amsterdam and smoked hash. And then we went to Munich and drank beer. And then we went to Prague and tripped out. Prague was so romantic. And then we went to Italy and saw the *David*. . . .' So many Americans do that.

"The message I would want to put out is how much it meant to me just to do it on my own. The hardest part is leaving the United States and getting the money together. You might have supportive parents, but you might not be able to say, 'Dad, I need some money. I'm going to Argentina by myself, and I'm going to learn more than I would if I went through a university.' Parents are used to writing checks to institutions, not ideas.

"There's nothing like being in a tiny Honduran town, eating pineapple and watching the chickens fight. Or if you're in a rain forest, and it hits you that nature is a total miracle. The parrots and tarantulas aren't there for me to see them; they're just there.

"How can you communicate that to somebody? All you can say is, it's worth it. It will be that good if you do it. Just give yourself enough credit to try."

Eric has since graduated from Berkeley and stuck around to earn a Ph.D. in agricultural and resource economics at the University of California at Davis. "I was looking at what kind of graduate school would pay for more international travel," he said. He lived in Mexico for eighteen months doing survey work for his dissertation, then came back to the United States after finishing his degree. He worked as an international economist for the U.S. Department of Agriculture for a year and is now working at UC Davis again and also consulting on projects based in Rome that involve the international exchange of seeds.

"While I wonder if I will ever again be able to strap on a backpack and wander the world for months at a time, I know that there are lessons that I learned during my time off that I carry with me every day."

For more information . . .

See General Resources, Travel/Outdoor Adventure page 244.

Part 4

Travel

Ted Conover
AMHERST COLLEGE
Rode freight trains with hoboes

As a college kid riding the freight trains with railroad hoboes twice his age, Ted Conover often stuck out.

When he tried to explain, half truthfully usually, what he was doing, the tramps generally took him at his word. "Well, I used to be a student at a college out east, but I grew tired of that life. I heard there were still guys riding the rails, and that had always seemed pretty interesting to me, so I thought I'd come check it out for myself," he told them.

Early on in his adventure, however, one reflective tramp caught the irony. "Young man," he said, laughing, "this will be your education!"

Ted was twenty-two when he left Amherst College in 1980 to ride the freight trains. The conversation above comes from *Rolling Nowhere* (Penguin, 1982), the book Ted wrote about his year on the rails.

Ted eventually became a successful magazine writer, and he has written several books since *Rolling Nowhere*. Never, however, did he envision a career evolving directly from his time off. "I never imagined when I set off that I might write a book. Certainly, I'd never met anyone except some professors who had written a book. I think I hadn't been brought up to be that ambitious," he recalled.

Ted grew up in Denver, where as a white student he found himself bused across town to a black high school the city was attempting to integrate. "Amherst was socially homogeneous, which I wasn't used to. And performance standards were very high. All of it was a bit jarring.

"It was the beginning of my sophomore year when I started feeling restless, thinking that there must be more to life than this.

"I was being asked to choose my major, which would presumably influence my choice of career, but I'd really done nothing my whole life except go to school. How, if school is your main experience in the world, are you supposed to know what you want to do in the world after school?

"For all the advantages Amherst had—and the ivory tower has many—a disadvantage can be the lack of exposure to other people and other places. So I didn't feel like I was leaving education when I left Amherst; I felt that I was leaving to broaden my education."

Ted left college to live in Dallas for a year with VISTA (Volunteers in Service to America), which was a sort of precursor to today's AmeriCorps program. "A lot of my friends were planning junior years abroad, and I considered that, but I had always been struck by how many of my friends knew more about Europe than about the United States. I thought I could spend junior year at home, if you will, and just not get credit for it.

"We were doing community organizing to empower the lower-income people there. That was the line, and it was mostly true." Ted worked in a Dallas neighborhood, and his duties included organizing tenants, running crime-prevention programs, and working with teens. VISTA paid just enough to sustain the modest standard of living he had been accustomed to as a student.

Ted returned to Amherst a more focused student and a more focused person. "After fifteen months, I was ready to go back. I had a better idea of what I wanted, and socially I had a better idea of who I was and where I fit in, of what mattered and what didn't. I declared an anthropology major, and I moved off campus. My grades, which had been so-so, started a steady climb after I returned."

As Ted read more anthropology, however, the wanderlust began to nip at his heels once more. Ever since he was a child, he had been fascinated by railroad hoboes. Slowly, he began to imagine what it might be like to study them.

After reading a few ancient books on hobo life and a smattering of magazine and newspaper articles from the previous ten years, Ted said it became clear that no one had done much recent anthropological fieldwork on hoboes. The lack of work, he later wrote in his thesis on railroad hoboes, almost made it seem as if the hobo way of life had died out sometime during the middle of the twentieth century.

But Ted had a hunch that hoboes were still around. "I didn't think they were dying off, and I justified the sort of romantic idea of riding the rails as a worthwhile activity, because anthropology made me think that I wouldn't just be riding for fun and adventure. I'd be riding to learn and observe and maybe later to bear witness in some way to what I had seen and heard."

Ted's suggestion that he might "bear witness" to hobo culture in the form of an undergraduate honors thesis struck his professors as somewhat mad. While they didn't rule it out, they generally discouraged Ted with the observation that it was a highly dangerous thing to do. "One professor asked whether I had considered the possibility of homosexual rape out there," Ted said.

"VISTA didn't seem to worry my parents too much, but this did. They had never stopped me from doing anything since I was fifteen, but my mother was worried about my safety. My father, on the other hand, seemed to have a suspicion that this was an elaborate way of goofing off. Some of my friends were also skeptical. 'Why would hoboes want to talk to a guy like you?' they asked me.

"But in a way that sort of discouragement was a source of inspiration. You just get to the point where you want to show them that you can make it happen."

So that fall Ted avoided the crowds of back-to-school shoppers at the mall and went to the Salvation Army store instead.

"How did tramps look? Taking a calculated guess, I outfitted myself with secondhand clothing, let my hair grow long, grew a beard, and got dirty," he wrote in his thesis. "I carried a small used shoulder bag (for my notes, tape recorder, and other valuables) and a bedroll.

"Figuring the best place to meet tramps was near trains, and that an understanding of trains was necessary to living their life, I got on the rails as soon as possible.

"It was not easy. Unfamiliar with the workings of railroad yards, of the freedom the tramp may have in them and the etiquette he must observe, it took me two days after meeting that first tramp to 'catch out' of St. Louis for Kansas City, and two more days to actually arrive there."

Though Ted quickly got better at hopping freights, trying to relate to the tramps that he met along the way was never easy. While he did all the same things they did—sleeping in shelters, exploiting the welfare system, and selling his blood—the line between Ted Conover and the account he gave of himself was admittedly somewhat fuzzy.

"It was an intense experiment in self-identity," he recalled. "I think anytime you willingly relocate yourself and plop yourself down in a different cultural milieu, you're going to have that.

"I wasn't always free to tell people who I was or where I came from. Sometimes it put me in peril, so I would keep things to myself that might have been better spoken about for my own peace of mind.

"It was incredibly important to me to be accepted by these people who were not like me, so I would hide parts of myself in order to be accepted by them. I think most anthropologists do this. In fact, I think many people who are members of a minority have to do it too, and it works on all kinds of different levels."

While passing through his hometown for the first time, Ted was arrested on a bridge. The president of the United States was in town, and the Denver police had been told not to allow any derelicts on the bridge. Ted was charged with disobeying a police officer's order: "Hurry up, asshole!" to be exact.

"'Man,' I thought, 'would I love to tell him a thing or two,'" Ted wrote in *Rolling Nowhere*. "The name of my college would be a good place to start . . . and then I might just mention that my dad headed up a big law firm downtown—ever heard of it? No? Well, you're gonna, you bastard. Just as soon as I get to a telephone, somebody's head's gonna roll."

But then he stopped himself. "It would be too easy. Revenge would be sweet, but it would prove nothing. I would show only that I wasn't what I appeared to be. That was the opposite of my objective: to let people believe I was somebody else and see how I was treated, see what life was like from the other side. It had gotten a bit tough, and I was ready to give up." So, instead of calling his father, Ted spent the night in jail.

The reward for his perseverance came midway through his journey, as he approached a man dismantling a boxcar for firewood on the outskirts of a small town.

"Hey," the man asked. "You a tramp?"

"What?"

"I said, 'Are you a tramp?'"

Few questions could have caught me so off-guard. . . . This struck right at the heart of the matter.

"Yeah," I answered, too defensively. "I guess I am." I was amazed at how close the words came to ringing true. In part because my desire was so strong, the jungles were becoming my home. For weeks I had been concerned with appearances. . . . When tramps looked at me, would they see themselves. . . . But now I saw that I had neglected what was going on inside. Sloughing off that feeling of being an *outsider . . . was essential to achieving the ease of mind and manners that would make tramps see me as one of them. "Yeah, I guess I am," I had said and it struck me that, to a degree, saying it had made it so.*

As his time on the rails wore on, however, Ted also felt the need to differentiate himself from the tramps. "At night I would steal away to brush my teeth, just to remind myself that I had teeth and I planned to keep them, whereas a lot of the hoboes didn't have them anymore."

He also called his friends collect, partly to remind himself that there were people who would pay to talk to him.

Those phone calls, however, were sometimes a source of anxiety. As Ted explained in his book, near the end of his trip, he called his college roommate to voice some of his frustrations.

Trying to be helpful, his roommate told him to look on the bright side: Ted could rest easy now, knowing that if anything ever went really wrong, he could still get by as a tramp.

The remark, only partly serious, had been intended as a comfort, but it had entirely the opposite effect. Hearing someone who knew me propose trampdom as a conceivable destiny for me was utterly depressing. . . . In a complete turnabout from my earlier concerns, I wanted a guarantee that, while I could get close to tramps, I could never really become one. . . . I wanted someone I knew to say that going native sounded more absurd to them than it did to me right now.

It was at that point that Ted realized it was time to start winding his way back to Denver. His homecoming was to be a surprise. He did not tell his family when he would be arriving, in the hope that they might not recognize him when he finally rang the doorbell.

And, sure enough, they didn't. "Some things can probably be imagined without too many details. Double-takes are such a movie cliché, but this was a true classic. My sister came to the door, and I asked for Mrs. Conover.

She said to wait just a minute, but a few seconds later she turned around and whispered, 'Ted?' It was wonderful."

Ted returned to Amherst that winter with 450 pages of notes and observations. Safe and sound, he was welcomed with open arms by the professors in the anthropology department, who helped him mold his research on the American hobo into a thesis that won him the highest possible honors.

Reintegrating into life at Amherst was not as difficult as Ted had anticipated. "I was a bit nervous about returning to college, because there's a hobo part of me that likes the idea of freedom from schedules and deadlines, and college is all about schedules and deadlines," he said.

"Because I was working on my own so much that last semester, school wasn't as bad as I thought it would be. I was an independent scholar, essentially an interdisciplinary hobo major. When hoboes became my thesis, I could talk about my experiences as well as my work when we sat around the tables in the dining hall. So it wasn't ultimately as alienating as it might have been."

Ted wrote an article about his experiences on the rails for the Amherst alumni magazine that spring. A few days after it came out, he was interviewed by an Associated Press reporter who had seen his story. In the remarkable sequence of events that followed, the AP story went out over the national wires, and Ted received interview requests from the *Today* show, *Good Morning America*, and National Public Radio. "It was such a riot. So surreal," he said.

Luckily, the calls didn't start coming in until a few days after he had finished his thesis. Looking back on what he had written, however, Ted realized that there was another story lurking between the lines of his ethnography: his own.

While he was in New York appearing on the *Today* show, Ted met with a literary agent who happened to have grown up near one of the largest railroad yards in the country. Within three weeks, the agent had sold Ted's book proposal for *Rolling Nowhere*.

"I had to call the *Indianapolis Star*, because I was supposed to work for them that summer, to tell them that I might need to take a few long weekends to meet with an editor in New York," he recalled. "And they just said no, if you feel like you're going to need that many days, you should let someone more deserving have the internship.

"I had never walked away from a job before, but at that point I did. By then I had this odd new job, which is what I still do: writing for myself. I'm a self-employed writer."

It's been twenty years now since Ted last lived on the rails, but he said that some of the lessons he learned as a hobo have stuck.

"In the best of all possible worlds, you're not just a kid and then an adult," he explained. "Growing up is not something that ends when you leave college. On the rails, I came to understand identity as a mutable thing. I have a strong sense of who I am, but I also know that that sense changes, and I have almost come to expect to see it change.

"Profound change is possible at any point in your life, perhaps even desirable. If you're going to *live*, in italics, at the highest pitch possible, you have to be ready to try something completely different.

"I hope my experience isn't isolated. I think that one of the greatest things about the extended adolescence in this country is that, with luck, you can take some chances; you can do something that wasn't in the plans for you.

"Who knows? It could be a waste of time, but it could be something you'll always remember. For me, it totally shifted the direction of my life, and I think what a huge mistake it would have been not to take those chances."

After years of being out of print, Vintage Books recently revived *Rolling Nowhere*. Though Ted now has kids of his own, he still enjoys parachuting into interesting, dangerous places and writing about what he finds there. *Newjack*, his first-person account of working as a prison guard at Sing-Sing, came out in 2000. And in 2001, Amherst College, where his professors begged him to stay in school and off the rails, gave him an honorary degree.

For more information . . .

See General Resources, Travel/Outdoor Adventure, Travel/Outdoor Adventure in the United States, page 244.

Corey Flournoy
UNIVERSITY OF ILLINOIS
Traveled around the United States as the first black
national president of FFA

As an African American eighth-grader living on the south side of Chicago, attending a magnet school that specialized in the agricultural sciences didn't seem like a possibility to Corey Flournoy. But when it was the only high school that accepted him, he didn't have much of a choice about going there.

Strange as it was, Corey's now grateful that things worked out the way they did. "It was the single biggest thing that changed my life and made it what it is today," he said.

"It was an interesting opportunity to do something besides just sitting in class," Corey recalled. "It was very much hands-on learning, a different side of how things are done. We weren't just learning about different cuts of meat, say, but we'd go down to Jewel, the grocery store, to see how the animal got cut up."

As a condition of enrollment with the high school, Corey had to sign up for membership with the Future Farmers of America (now known as FFA), a national youth organization that supports the career aspirations of students enrolled in agricultural education programs. FFA has an elaborate network of local, state, and national leadership programs, and Corey became the president of his school's chapter in his senior year.

"I had never been athletic growing up," he said. "I was always the last one chosen for the games in elementary school. I'd never been that competitive. But FFA gave me a chance to excel in the nonsports arena. They had a ton of contests. They called them 'career development events,' like dairy cattle judging or agricultural sales contests to try to sell the most of a product of some sort. There was a parliamentary procedure contest too, which I won first place in at the state level.

"As I became active in the organization, I got to thinking that I would love to be a statewide officer, which would have meant taking a year away from school before college. My mother was anything but enthused. It wasn't so much the organization that was the problem, but having to miss time from school."

Still, she might have wondered about the organization. It was sixty-five years old and had never had an African American state officer before, or an officer from an urban area. "It was my true first experience that proved that even in current times, racism is still alive and well," Corey recalled. "I ran [up] against a lot of negative comments. I still have the video of the runoff vote, when people abstained rather than vote against the candidate who was in a runoff with me."

Nevertheless, Corey was elected vice president of the Illinois chapter—one of five people who were elected to statewide office. They spent the next year traveling around the state giving motivational speeches, conducting workshops and seminars, and going to awards banquets. "I was based out of my home, but I was gone 250 days that year," he said. "There was no way I could have gone to school or held down a job. I didn't have my own car, so my mother took out a loan to buy me one, and I paid her back." While Corey wasn't paid for his service, he did get meal money and mileage reimbursement.

When he was traveling, he generally stayed with host families, which was an education for everyone involved. "I was treated well in every household," he recalled. "It was interesting for the families I stayed with. They all wanted to talk, because most of them had never had a black person stay with them before."

And those were the families that were willing to host him. "I did not get very many requests to speak in southern Illinois," he said. "What I learned about racism and how it operates was that people who don't like you just stay away from you. If they didn't request [for] you to come, you didn't deal with it. I didn't have to suffer being called a nigger. Still, my friends would tell me about things people were saying behind my back. I grew a lot spiritually that year, just praying for my safety and my sanity."

Corey began his freshman year at the University of Illinois with a vow to spend a year away from FFA to concentrate on his studies. He joined an agricultural fraternity and moved in to the frat house, but once again, he found himself as the odd man out. And this time he wasn't just visiting for the night. "I quickly realized that there was a difference between going to a household and visiting with families versus actually living in that environment," he said. "Eventually, you can't fake niceness. There were a couple of members who didn't want a nigger living in their house, and they said that to my face. That wasn't the most disappointing part, as much as the fact that other people in the house didn't stand up for me. It's supposed to be a sense of brotherhood, and I wasn't feeling it."

Outside the frat house, however, Corey had built a pretty big fan club. His run as vice president of the Illinois chapter of FFA was so successful that people were urging him to run for national office. "I knew I had support outside of the state," he said. "There'd only been three national officers who were black, and never one from an urban area. But I felt like in the national elections it might be an asset—that it would help me stand out."

He needed all the help he could get, since the elections for national president were tough. Corey spent six months preparing, and a friend tutored him. The voting process was unlike most political campaigns. "It's very similar to the Miss America pageant," Corey said. "Each state gets to submit one candidate, and once you get the nomination from your state, there are six interviews testing everything ranging from group dynamics to agricultural and educational issues to your presentation skills."

Corey ended up with the crown and sash when his name was called in front of 30,000 people at the FFA national convention in Kansas. "Then I was bombarded," he recalled. "It was this freak story, this black guy from Chicago as president of a traditionally white organization. A novelty story. Every newspaper had an article: *The New York Times, USA Today,* the Associated Press. It was something I never expected or even considered."

The most shocking media mention came one Friday soon afterward. "I was in a hotel in Chicago to speak," Corey recalled. "I was flipping through the TV channels while getting ready and stopped on HBO. Dennis Miller does this thing where he takes clippings from the week and make jokes about them. There were a few Bill Clinton jokes, and then lo and behold, there he was, with a clipping with a picture of me and my mother. He said that when they interviewed me about my goals for the year, I said that my major goal was to help soybean growers, but that all cotton farmers should go to hell!

"I just sat there thinking, 'This is not really happening, is it?'"

But it was, and Corey needed to take another year off from school to serve. "This time it was different, though," he said. "I was gone 317 days instead of 250, but it was totally paid for. The other national officers and I were based in Alexandria, Virginia, but most of the time we weren't together. We'd travel around giving speeches and doing workshops, attending conferences and events as special guests.

"I became an adult overnight. I didn't have a choice. I sat on the board of the national FFA organization and spent a lot of time talking to CEOs from different corporations. Here I was twenty-one years old sitting on the board with the CEO of John Deere. I was talking to individuals who had enough money to buy and sell my family. It was an incredible experience. Even looking back now it's hard to believe that a black kid from Chicago had an opportunity to do this. It was a true blessing."

After a year as the center of attention, Corey's confidence grew enormously. By the time he returned to the University of Illinois, he knew he had built some skills that he could use professionally. "When I came back to school, rather than hanging out I was still traveling around, but this time it was for myself, making money," he explained.

"Instead of going to a lot of parties and bars, I formed a business doing speeches and workshops with a friend of mine. It was called Creative Outreach. We charged $200 for a twenty-minute speech, which was good money for college students. We got one contract to train middle management at a company in Des Moines on how to write and give a presentation. Most people give boring presentations in the workplace. I remember going in and thinking that it was crazy, but it worked."

In fact, it worked well enough that that company continued to call on Corey over the next few years to help with its training. Word of his speaking and teaching prowess spread, and for several years after he graduated he worked and traveled on the weekends continuing his efforts with Creative Outreach. During the week he worked at Leo Burnett, a well-regarded advertising agency in Chicago, first as an account executive with clients like Altoids and later in human resources.

Eventually, however, Corey took a buyout from the agency when the economy soured. "It was a cool job, but my heart wasn't in it," he said. "What I enjoyed most about my time with FFA was helping people. That's what I'd always planned on doing." Today he's giving speeches and seminars full-time on leadership development and other skills. "It's frightening," he said of the pressures of working for himself without a safety net underneath him. "Some days I want to give up and go work for Corporate America again."

Still, all of his business has come in by word of mouth so far, and he made a decent living even in the worst part of the recession. "When all is said and done, I don't think my quality of life has changed," he said. "I'm more conscious about money, but I have a lot more freedom. I wouldn't change anything in terms of the way things have happened. Had I not had a rough time in state office, I never would have gotten the national FFA office. The first experience humbled me, and that made me even more grateful for the opportunities I had later."

For more information . . .

www.ffa.org—The official site of the FFA provides a great depth and breadth of information on almost everything FFA, from student programs like the New Century Farmer—where you (the farmer) will learn how to profit from technology—to newly available internships. Information on joining FFA and student discussion boards are accessible from the site. You can buy snappy FFA suspenders here, too.

Miles Gilliom
BROWN UNIVERSITY
Hiked the Appalachian Trail with his dog, Merlin

As a teenager growing up in a house filled with four siblings and two cousins, Miles Gilliom often felt the need for a quiet hike alone in the woods behind his house. But his love for the outdoors had been cultivated long before his house got so crowded.

"My parents have always been interested in the outdoors, and we did a fair amount of camping when I was little. I also went to a day camp, and once a summer we would take an overnight trip. The counselors there displayed a real reverence for the woods, and that was something that I wanted to emulate."

Although Miles occasionally brought his mom along on his treks through the woods, he usually went by himself. "I think that's always been my nature. Given the choice to be in a large group setting or on my own, I would often take the latter."

Miles made an exception for his dog, Merlin, who was always up for a walk. The dog was one thing that didn't get shared in the Gilliom house; Miles's father, who worked in marketing for IBM at the time, and his mother, a counselor in private practice, bought him the dog for his fourteenth birthday.

Miles chose to attend Brown University. "Suddenly I was at a school where people had parents who were CEOs of corporations and doctors and lawyers. I guess I was feeling like a lot of people had had a lot more exposure than I had to the world," he said.

"I think I was so excited about the prospect of going to Brown that I didn't spend enough time thinking about what I might find when I got there. And I immediately found myself overloaded with course work and not really knowing how to make decisions in terms of charting my academic future."

Miles first began to consider time off as his freshman year concluded. "Freshman year was really up and down. I was beginning to think that one of the things that I wanted to do was to step back from the pace my life was taking and just reassess a bit."

Miles elected to return for his sophomore year, but a painful ending to a romantic relationship and a particularly difficult year as a dorm counselor convinced him that his initial hunch had been correct.

He considered enrolling in an organized trek/academic semester in Nepal through the School for International Training, but he ultimately decided against it. "I eventually decided that I was more interested in doing something on my own, having some time where I would really be making my own choices. I think I felt I had just been responding for a long time, especially at school."

During his sophomore year, Miles and a few friends had spent three days hiking the Appalachian Trail, the continuous path that runs through the mountains from Maine to Georgia. After that trip, Miles was convinced that taking a longer, solo trek down the trail would be the best way to spend a semester away from Brown. And of course, Merlin would come along.

Miles had camped with his parents when he was younger and been on plenty of day hikes, but his knowledge of how to prepare for a mega-journey was limited. "There was just an underlying feeling of anxiety about the whole thing, not having any idea what it would be like to be in a tent fifty miles from the nearest town. Putting energy into making arrangements was a big way of allaying the anxiety aroused by taking on a new way of life, and I think I gained so much from just deciding to throw myself into it. Whatever you do, do it with gusto," he said.

"There is a whole community of people who have hiked the AT, people who are really willing to talk about their experiences, and I think they were probably the best resources. I met one person who worked in an outdoors store and had taken time off to spend three months on the AT. He gave me a lot of advice in terms of what kind of weather to expect, what kind of gear would be best, how to feed myself, and how much I could expect to spend." Miles also called the Appalachian Mountain Club, which has a wealth of resources for people planning to hike the trail.

As for equipment, Miles was basically starting from scratch. He needed boots, a tent, a camping stove, a sleeping bag, and a golden retriever–size knapsack. "I bought the best equipment I could find. After equipment costs and paying for the plane ticket up to Maine, I ended up spending about a dollar a mile for my 700-mile trip," which was about average at the time, he said.

Miles's college scholarship from IBM entitled him to a summer job there, so he signed on for a well-paying post to pay off his equipment debts. "I just decided that earning lots of money was going to be the main focus of the summer," he said.

When he was not on the job or playing with his band, the Porchhonkys, Miles was training for his expedition. "I went on a couple of camping trips to really get acquainted with my gear. I did a fair amount of running and some training hikes, where I would load my pack with forty pounds of books and just walk around the woods for three to four hours," he recalled.

As his departure date got closer, Miles began to think about what he wanted to accomplish in the seventy-five days he planned to spend on the trail. As he explained it, however, he came to realize that "goals" might be more of an obstacle than a focus. "I wanted to shift my emphasis from the 'goal' to the process and to make the process become the goal. Leaving things open, so that I would be closed to nothing. And I think that was enforced by what I found in living that way: that things could be more wonderful than I ever planned them to be."

Before Miles left, a friend gave him a journal. "There were so many things that lent themselves to journal writing. The experiences were so new and rich that it was very easy to write," he said.

Miles and Merlin arrived in Maine in mid-September, armed only with a sign saying "Two hikers going to Appalachian Trail," which was a good hundred miles away from the airport. A couple picked them up almost immediately and drove thirty miles out of their way to drop the campers at the beginning of the trail.

Miles's decision to start in September and hike from the north to the south were slightly out of the ordinary. Most people start in March in the south and finish early in the fall. Miles knew he wouldn't be hiking the entire trail, and since he started in September, he needed to hike away from the cold weather.

"The first stretch of trail is called the hundred-mile wilderness. It's by far the most isolated part of the trail. It really was a trial by fire. There are no chances to resupply, so I was carrying a week's worth of my own food and of Merlin's food."

AT hikers tend to be a food-preoccupied bunch, and Miles was no exception. He had shopped for most of his food before he left Georgia and left it packed in boxes for his parents to ship to post offices along his intended route. He would receive a two-week-supply box from home, put half the food in his pack, then send the other half to a post office farther south, where he could pick it up a week later.

"Basically, you can't eat enough when you're hiking, so the stops on the trail are really essential. Walking fifteen to twenty miles a day with a full pack, you burn the same amount of calories as you would running two full marathons. I'd try to find a Shoney's or some other all-you-can-eat restaurant and just settle down and chow to get my calories back up. I'd also buy food along the way, good packable stuff like peanut butter and candy bars."

For Merlin, eating was also something of a ritual. "I had Science Diet dog food, really high-performance stuff for him. But after the first ten days, it was clear that he wasn't getting enough. I started buying extra ramen noodles and mixing it in with his food. It would make this nice stew, which he just loved. He was so funny. He'd wait for it to cool, then pick up the whole bowl in his mouth and carry it off into the woods out of sight. I'd hear this chomping sound, and then he would come back about ten minutes later with a fat belly. Then he'd plop right down and sleep for about fourteen hours.

"He really was a great companion. I think his tolerance level was pretty similar to mine. I wouldn't always pay such close attention to how I was feeling or whether or not it would be good to stop and rest or get some food in my body. So, if he was looking pretty miserable, I'd stop and realize I wasn't feeling so great myself."

Miles and Merlin tended to set their clocks by the sun. "We would get into camp about an hour before the sun went down to set up and cook dinner. Some nights we'd be asleep by seven and we wouldn't wake up until six the next morning, eleven hours later," he said. "We tended to camp out if the weather was nice, and if it looked like rain, we'd shoot for a shelter." The Appalachian Mountain Club maintains many shelters on the trail.

"I was really happy out there. The day was pretty simple. I'd spend my time walking or looking at the map or reading or sleeping. I thought a lot about my connections at Brown and my place at Brown. I thought about my whole life. I tried to go back to my earliest memories and then through elementary school and high school. I thought about my dreams. There was also a lot of time when I was just looking around at the places I was passing through. I realized that I had never had that kind of control before, ever, over my own day."

Occasionally, however, Miles found his path blocked. "We had reached the summit of a mountain, and we heard something coming our way. Merlin froze, and there was a huge bull moose with a monster set of antlers about twenty feet ahead. Merlin barged past me to show the moose who was boss, and he almost got out a bark when it bared its teeth and charged right at us. I got into a stand of trees and Merlin just got the heck out."

Most of Miles's trail encounters were a bit less harrowing. All sorts of characters are out hiking the trail at any given time, but one of his favorites was a man named Vagabond Lou. "He's about seventy now, and I think he's hiked the AT four or five times. He's been struck by lightning three times and been body-searched by a full-grown bear. A pretty crazy old man, an incredible person."

As a general rule, however, Miles and Merlin hiked alone. One night Miles wrote in his journal:

I think this is the first day in my entire life where I haven't seen another human being. It is a quiet way to live and filled with possibilities. There is no self-consciousness in being alone, but much consciousness. Will I be able to remember that when I get back into the world of other people? God, I hope so.

Miles's parents had been supportive all along, and their only request was that he call home every so often. "It was interesting when I called home, the difficulty of going from acting as an individual to being part of a family. I'd feel myself slipping back into my one-of-nine modes and felt frustrated trying to express what I was feeling and experiencing. They were supportive, but I think they had no idea what it was like."

Miles finally got the chance to share his experiences when his dad joined him for a weekend on the trail. Miles had found a ride from Vermont to Virginia with a woman he had met on the trail. His dad met him a week later for a few days of hiking and dropped him and Merlin off in North Carolina to hike the rest of the trail on their own. They finished just before Thanksgiving, and Miles returned to Brown in January.

By the time Miles made it back to Rhode Island, he was flat broke. "I had been able to save a lot of money from my summer job, but I spent it all. It was a pretty lean semester. That's something to think about. I spent so much time focusing on paying for my time away that I didn't think too much about what would come after.

"I think that some of the jubilation of the trip faded with time. Since then, it has helped to go back to the journal. I was happy to find out that upon returning, I really could continue 'to live deliberately' to a certain extent. Obviously, I had a lot of things I had to do—writing papers and taking tests—but could make each class much more personal."

Eventually, Miles chose to help others cope with their own questions and personal issues and enrolled in a Ph.D. program to study psychology. While he still hikes from time to time, he says his time off has had the most lasting impact simply in the way he's chosen to live his life since. "At my own pace and on my own schedule," he said.

"The choice to take time off and the way you fill the time is such a personal one. I was really lucky to stumble into what was ideal for me. Just having my own time, my own space, was really what I needed."

It was a slow sad walk down the mountain. And a cold hungry one too. But these woods are here, waiting for our return. So much we learned and experienced among the trees and the mountains of Appalachia over the last five months. We will be back for sure. What lies in the future, we don't know, but we will find out.

Signed,
Miles and Merlin,
mountain explorers extraordinaire

For more information . . .

See General Resources, Travel/Outdoor Adventure, Travel/Outdoor Adventure in the United States, page 244.

Abigail Marble
BROWN UNIVERSITY
Rode her bike across the United States

When Abigail Marble briefly considered taking time off after finishing high school in Lake Oswego, a suburb of Portland, Oregon, she found herself swimming upstream. "Everybody around me was taking the SAT, writing essays, applying to colleges, going through interviews. It was all the stuff I dreaded," she said.

"I wondered what it would feel like to be stuck in Portland living at home when all my friends went off to college. I have always gotten along well with my parents, but it would have been hard to be as independent as I felt I needed to be if I was still living at home. The most immediate way to become more independent was to go to college."

Abigail matriculated at Brown University, across the country in Providence, Rhode Island. "The amount of activities in college was overwhelming. I went to meetings for this and meetings for that. I wrote an article here and did an illustration there."

By the time she made it to the summer after her sophomore year, Abigail yearned for a break to allow her to form a better idea of what she wanted to be getting out of Brown. She started tossing around ideas with Matt, a friend from high school, and together they resolved to ride their bikes across America.

"I spent the rest of the summer working a seven-hour morning shift in a coffee shop. After work, I biked to get in shape."

The trip was not expensive. "People absolutely can do an expedition like this. It's totally affordable. During the trip itself, we basically only spent money on food, which amounted to roughly ten dollars a day. As for what we spent on equipment before we left, our philosophy was less is more and cheaper is better.

"We started out with a two-person tent, sleeping bags, rain gear, a bike-repair kit, and a stove named Oscar because it was so grouchy. We packed John Steinbeck's *Travels with Charlie*, and kept trading books with people as we went along."

By mid-trip, Abigail was in phenomenal shape. "We averaged about seventy miles a day, with a few hundred-mile days thrown in."

The ride gave her lots of time to think. "If you want a chance to reflect about your life, get on a bike and ride for eight hours every day. Thirty percent of the time, I was thinking, 'Oh, my God. I'm so tired,' or 'My knee hurts,' but that's to be expected.

"The West Coast and the Midwest were one big outdoor adventure. The scenery was monumentally beautiful. As we approached the East Coast, it became more of an experience of meeting people."

Abigail came up with ingenious ways to encourage strangers to lend her and Matt a helping hand. "We stayed with a lot of strangers that we met on the road. We would bike up to people and ask if they knew if there was a park somewhere in town where we could camp out. Usually when you ask somebody that, they at least let you camp in their yard. Sometimes they even let you have a shower.

"Being on a bike makes a big difference. People are immediately interested in you and where you're from and what you're doing. And you don't look threatening when you're on a bicycle."

The biking duo sometimes found help in unexpected places. "We went into a doughnut shop and someone said, 'Oh, you're on a bike trip? Do you want to be on the radio?'

"So we went on the radio and talked about our trip for a little bit. We mentioned that we hoped to make it to Warsaw, Missouri, that night. Just as we were getting off the air, someone called the station and said, 'We live in Warsaw. Come and stay with us if you make it here.' It was great."

When they made it to Warsaw, Abigail said she was reminded of how unusual her adventure seemed to some people. "The woman we stayed with was shocked that I had the freedom to do this. On her wall, she had her high school graduation certificate, a portrait of her senior prom, and her wedding photo. I looked closer at her high school diploma. She had graduated the year after me. And they were trying to have children."

Abigail said most people assumed she and Matt were married. Others were puzzled as to why she had chosen to bike such a long way. "Lots of people asked me, 'Your parents let you do this?'

"My only fear was not knowing ahead of time where I was going to sleep, but I was continually surprised by how easy it was. We once knocked on someone's door and asked if we could camp on their lawn. They said sure, and then insisted on taking us out to dinner that night and breakfast the next morning."

Most people don't take such a freewheeling approach to their life—and their life's work—once they're grown up. But Abigail is an exception, though an increasingly common one. Today she's a freelance graphic designer and children's book illustrator, moving from project to project, not working exclusively for any single client.

"Taking time off had a big abstract influence," she said. "Just having that experience in my past has helped me appreciate independence and risk-taking . . . two big factors in the life of a freelancer. The bike trip sometimes strikes me as an early indicator of the choices I've made since then: to get off the beaten path, to pursue my own route on my own schedule, and to cross each bridge as I come to it apparently is my path in life.

"Freelancing makes me crazy sometimes, but it's clear that I'm drawn to it. The bike trip helped me to articulate that to myself. It turns out there aren't many points in life when it's that easy to take six months to just do something you've always wanted to do. The experience really changed the way I thought about myself."

Her only regret: "I actually wish I'd taken more time to balance my travel experience in this country with some time in a foreign country."

For more information . . .

www.adv-cycling.org—The Adventure Cycling Association is unquestionably the best place online to plan and outfit oneself for a bike tour across the country in any direction. And it should be. These were the people, after all, who mapped the TransAmerica Trail, an east-west route of back roads across the continental United States, way back in the 1970s. You'll also be able to find any other resources of any value to the cycling enthusiast through the website.

Hillary Zazove

UNIVERSITY OF MONTANA
Camped in the Rockies with the National Outdoor Leadership School

---

The best thing about high school for Hillary Zazove was that it ended.

"I can honestly say I did not really learn anything in high school," she said. "I'm serious. I would testify to that. I think I came out of there dumber."

Attendance was not a priority. "I was barely attending school," she said. "If they said you can only miss ninety-two days, I would miss ninety-two days. I marked the days in my calendar." Going to college was also not a major concern. "I don't even know if the school had a college counselor," she said.

Certain that she wanted to get away from the classroom for a while but unsure of what to do, Hillary began to explore various options. She also wrestled with the concerns of her parents, who viewed not being in school as a risky proposition. "My dad didn't want to have to worry about me," she said.

During her final year at Niles North High School in Illinois, a family friend took an interest in her. "Mr. Baxter gave me a brochure about NOLS, the National Outdoor Leadership School. NOLS runs outdoor education and leadership training programs around the world. The thought of him giving me that brochure and having enough confidence in me to think that I should take it home and show my folks totally helped my self-esteem."

Hillary applied to NOLS's fall semester in the Rockies, one of their longer, more challenging, and more expensive courses. She was required to write an application essay and submit some financial documents to qualify for their scholarship program.

"It cost a lot," she said. "I paid for part of it, I got $2,000 deferred to pay off as a loan, and NOLS gave me $2,500 in scholarship money. My parents are both Chicago public school teachers, and they weren't making enough money to justify spending $6,000 on just one semester." The NOLS semester in the Rockies costs more than $8,000 these days.

After graduating from high school, Hillary lived at home and got a job working at a health club. Her goal was to make money until she began the NOLS trip in September. "My parents knew that I was being responsible and that I was trying to do something that was going to be positive for me."

The job meshed well with Hillary's growing passion for athletics. "To help get in shape for my trip, I was running all the time and lifting weights. I felt really good about myself."

Meanwhile, reports from her friends who had gone off to college did not make Hillary feel that she was missing much. "They were like 'Oh, it's so cool. There's all these cute guys, everyone totally parties, I live in these dorms, the campus is really pretty, and the food sucks.'"

NOLS sent Hillary extensive information about how to prepare for the trip. They made packing suggestions, encouraged participants to exercise as much as possible, and included reading material about the areas where the group would be traveling.

Instead of spending lots of money on new camping gear, Hillary simply used the equipment that NOLS issues free to anyone who needs it. "You don't have to buy any of it, which makes the trip much more affordable," she said.

The fall semester in the Rockies provides students with a comprehensive introduction to technical outdoor skills. Hillary's trip included a mountain section, canyon hiking, winter skiing, caving, and rock climbing. The group learned basic wilderness living skills such as cooking, stove use and repair, map reading, route finding, and first aid. They then progressed to a study of plant and animal identification, geology, prehistoric Indian cultures, and the natural history of the area.

"We lived outdoors, prepared our own meals, and took care of ourselves," Hillary recalled. NOLS also emphasizes minimum-impact camping. Students are encouraged to leave no trace of their presence. The seventeen students in her group traveled in small groups of four to six to minimize their impact on the environment.

"We hiked seven to ten miles a day carrying backpacks that weighed over sixty-five pounds," she said. Initially, the groups included an instructor, but they later traveled alone.

Hillary was also able to do a "solo"—spend a day and a night alone in the wilderness. Members of her group who chose to do so were also able to go through the student-led expedition without food. The fasting section was designed to increase participants' confidence about their ability to survive if they find themselves stranded someday.

"We hiked through the canyon country of the Colorado Plateau in southern Utah. We came up over the top of a cliff and a huge expanse of land spread out below us. Our group had found a place called the Valley of the Gods. Huge mesas twenty miles apart rose up in incredible shapes and colors everywhere."

Each participant was required to keep a journal. Hillary wrote down what she was learning about plant and animal identification, the Anasazi culture, and the area's ecosystems. She also studied for, and successfully passed, NOLS's wilderness first-aid course; she was one of the few people on the trip to do so.

In the winter section of the semester, the group learned the basics of snow camping, skiing, avalanche safety, snow physics, cold-weather physiology, and winter ecology. "Winter section was really cold but it was fun. We built igloos and read Jack London stories by our lanterns at night."

Hillary believes that she came back from NOLS a changed person. "It wasn't until I got home that I realized what a big thing that had been for me. I knew I could basically learn anything if given the right opportunity.

"In high school, one of the reasons I didn't learn anything was that I kind of thought I was dumb. Maybe that's why I never even thought about college. I didn't think I had the potential to go to college and be successful."

Going on a NOLS trip gave Hillary an opportunity to test her abilities in a new environment. "I was with all these people who were taking time off from college. Many of them had been enrolled for a year or two, were doing NOLS, and then going back. I realized that I was at their level. I was capable of handling myself in very diverse situations. Challenging, technical situations, taking tests, learning wilderness first aid."

NOLS helped Hillary overcome the distaste for learning she had developed during an unrewarding high school career. "It was hands-on learning," she said. "It was not like sitting in a classroom with a teacher who you probably thought just went home and watched TV at night. It's hard to want to learn from someone you don't respect. I respected the NOLS instructors and wanted to hear what they had to say."

After successfully completing the NOLS course, Hillary was accepted at the University of Montana. She found it easy to incorporate what she had learned during her NOLS trip into her new college life. "I started an outdoors/camping/skiing group in the dorm to take advantage of what I had learned on my trip. I also became interested in endurance running and endurance cycling. And I started doing triathlons."

Hillary elected to pursue a communications major and has considered becoming a social worker. "I feel there are so many people out there who genuinely are not having their needs met. Women who are trying to get off welfare, or elderly people stuck in rest homes, for example. They're feeling unsatisfied, unfulfilled, frustrated, fed up, and angry. I want to be able to talk to them and try to help them meet their needs.

"NOLS gave me a huge confidence boost about school. I hung out with the healthy crowd, not with a bunch of partiers. We would do our homework. I wouldn't miss any classes. I would sit, listen, and take notes. I was a sponge for information. I was in really great physical and mental shape. I didn't resent going to class. It was my choice to be there."

For more information . . .

See General Resources, Travel/Outdoor Adventure, Travel/Outdoor Adventure in the United States, Programs, page 244.

General Resources

Work

Work in the United States

Temporary Work

Websites

www.jobsearchlink.com—Here you'll find a bulging plethora of temporary and job placement agencies—so many you'll have to take a day off just to do research here.

www.monster.com—If you don't know this one, you need to get online more. Most popular online recruitment site ever.

www.hotjobs.com—Second most popular site for online recruitment.

www.workindex.com—Offers a vast list of national staffing and temporary employment services.

www.vault.com—The home of Vault, Inc., the Insider Career Network. In its own words, "the Internet's ultimate destination for insider company information, advice, and career management services." That's pretty right on.

Publications

How to Be a Permanent Temp: Winning Strategies for Thriving in Today's Workplace, by Joan Damico. Career Press, Inc., 2001. Easy-to-follow guidebook for the permanent temporary (no pun intended) worker in today's constantly evolving economy. Includes chapters about resumes and cover letters, interviewing, and more.

The Temp Survival Guide: How to Prosper as an Economic Nomad of the Nineties, by Brian Hassett. Republica Books, 1999. The concise survival guide for the permanent temp worker.

What Color Is Your Parachute? A Practical Manual for Job Hunters and Career Changers, by Richard Nelson Bolles. Ten Speed Press, 1995. While most people call this a career book, it's a good read for anyone feeling generally confused about what the next twelve months or twelve years may hold.

Internships

Websites

www.internships.wetfeet.com—A massive search engine providing links to employers and career centers, with a large database of advertised internships.

www.dynamy.org—Dynamy is an internship program in Worcester, Massachusetts, for high school graduates. Participants live in Worcester and work in a variety of internships in the community over a nine-month period.

www.PrincetonReview.com—Our online internship database includes profiles and contact information for hundreds of the most competitive internships in the world.

Publications

The Internship Bible, by Mark Oldman and Samer Hamadeh, the creators of Vault, Inc. Random House, Inc., 2003. Precisely, a bible to be studied, using its expert advice from former interns, indexes, suggested tips, and company-specific information.

The Best 109 Internships, by Mark Oldman and Samer Hamadeh. Random House, Inc., 2000. Comprehensive guide with extensive reviews of the internships with the best quality of life and highest compensation spanning across the fruited plain.

Military

Websites

www.military.com—"Benefiting the U.S. Army, Navy, Air Force, Marine Corps." Provides links to military news updates, finance information, military careers, and other general military statistics and recruiting information.

www.defenselink.mil—Official website of the U.S. Department of Defense. Here you'll find numerous links to news updates, military history, military branch information, and job opportunities.

www.army.mil—Official website of the U.S. Army.

www.af.mil—Official website of the U.S. Air Force.

www.navy.mil—Official website of the U.S. Navy.

www.usmc.mil—Official website of the U.S. Marines.

Publication

The Real Insider's Guide to Military Basic Training: A Recruit's Guide of Advice and Hints to Make It Through Boot Camp, by Peter Thompson. Upublish.com, 1998. "Written for a new recruit by a recruit." Easy-to-read chapters offering helpful hints and advice on the ins and outs of basic training.

Environmental/Outdoor

Publications

Careers for Environmental Types and Others Who Respect the Earth, by Michael Fasulo and Jane Kinney. McGraw-Hill Professional, 2001. Explores the growing variety of environmental careers for people with all levels of experience and education.

The Environmental Career Guide: Job Opportunities with the Earth in Mind, by Nicholas Basta. John Wiley & Sons, Inc., 1991. Explores the vast number of career options in the field of preserving and protecting the environment. Contains chapters about the history of environmentalism, today's job market, and environmental business.

Programs

National Park Service. Seasonal and temporary jobs in national parks across the U.S. (202) 208-4648. www.nps.gov/personnel.

The Student Conservation Association. SCA interns work with federal land agencies and private natural-resource organizations. Ask for its publication, *Scan.* (603) 543-1700. www.sca-inc.org.

Conservation Directory. Lists organizations, agencies, and personnel engaged in conservation work and natural-resources use and management at state, national, and international levels. Also lists college and universities in the U.S. and Canada that have conservation studies programs. Published annually by the National Wildlife Federation. (202) 797-6800 or (800) 822-9919. www.nwf.org.

U.S. PIRG. The PIRGs (Public Interest Research Groups) offer some terrific research and lobbying opportunities, including door-to-door canvassing, collecting signatures for ballot initiatives, or helping with fund-raising for various environmental causes. Wages are at about subsistence level, but you'll generally have a neat bunch of coworkers. (202) 546-9707. www.uspirg.org.

The Environmental Careers Organization. ECO offers internship opportunities for current college students and recent graduates. It publishes *The New Complete Guide to Environmental Careers*, which gives a great overview of the field and also offers some valuable information on internships. Also sponsors the Environmental Placement Services program, which matches qualified candidates with paid internships. Ask for ECO's resource list, which details dozens of job opportunities with nonprofits, as well as clearinghouses for more information on jobs with environmental organizations. (617) 426-4783.

Friends of the Earth. Offers internships and fellowships for college and graduate students with an interest in environmental issues. Issues include ozone depletion, environmental justice, drinking water, World Bank development projects, chemical safety, corporate accountability, indigenous peoples' rights, trade, jobs, the environment, tax and federal budget reform, and more. (202) 783-7400. www.foe.org.

Work Abroad

General Resources

Publications

Job Surfing: Working Abroad: Using the Internet to Find a Job and Get Hired, by Erik Olson and Jim Blau. Random House, Inc., 2002. Includes invaluable chapters on how to post a resume or portfolio online, "the lowdown on more than 300 of the most relevant websites," and strategies for making the most of your time abroad.

How to Get a Job with a Cruise Line: Adventure-Travel-Romance: How to Sail Around the World on Luxury Cruise Ships & Get Paid for It, by Mary Fallon Miller. Ticket to Adventure, 2000. The title says it all. Includes tips from cruise-line employees.

Working on Cruise Ships, by Sandra Bow. Vacation-Work, 1999. "The definitive guide to finding work on the most popular cruise ships in the world, including Princess, Carnival, Royal Caribbean, Norwegian, and others." Describes more than 150 cruise-ship jobs.

Programs

People to People International. Arranges unpaid internships in London, Dublin, Moscow, Paris, Prague, and other foreign cities. (816) 531-4701.

Accord Cultural Exchange. Au pair placements in Austria, France, Germany, Italy, and Spain. ACE charges $1,200 for a full-year placement and $750 for a summer job. If your French is good enough (four years of high school French or a year or two of college study should suffice), ACE will find you an internship with a multinational company. (415) 386-6203. www.cognitext.com/accord.

Teaching English

Websites

www.teflcertificate.com—Official site of the Boston Language Institute and its TEFL (Teach English as a Foreign Language) program. This site offers access to program information and other resource links.

www.tesol.net—Lots of resources for prospective or current English teachers, with job listings sorted by country.

www.eslcareer.com—Links to available teaching jobs organized by regions of the world.

Publication

Teaching English in Asia: Finding a Job and Doing It Well, by Galen Harris Valle. Pacific View Press, 1995. Includes a helpful section with country-by-country guidelines. Also contains useful sections on what makes a good teacher and activities to do with your students.

Program

Japan Exchange Teaching Program. The Japanese government sponsors JET, offering one-year programs for assistant language teachers and coordinators for international relations. (202) 238-6772-3 for the embassy or (800) 463-6538 for an application. www.mofa.go.jp/j_info/visit/jet.

Volunteer/Community Service

Volunteer/Community Service in the United States

Programs

American Friends Service Committee. The AFSC is a Quaker organization with a list of volunteer service possibilities. (215) 241-7295. www.afsc.org.

USA Freedom Corps. Volunteer service program created by President George W. Bush involving opportunities in the government and nonprofit sectors. www.usafreedomcorps.gov.

Habitat for Humanity. Habitat builds affordable housing for low-income families. For information on local chapters, go to www.habitat.org.

Volunteers in Service to America. VISTA is now part of the federal government's Corporation for National Service. Participants live and work in communities where they help develop grassroots initiatives to assist the people who live there. Pay ranges from $600 to $800 per month, including health insurance, with a year-end bonus of about $4,725 to put toward higher education. www.friendsofvista.org.

Youth Service America. A national clearinghouse for information on youth service in the United States. It can put you in touch with service projects in your geographic area. (202) 296-2992. www.ysa.org.

Volunteer/Community Service Abroad

www.ivpsf.com—The International Volunteer Program promotes volunteering in Europe and the United States. The website offers program descriptions, resource links, former participants' feedback, and general program information.

www.unv.org—Official website for the United Nations Volunteers. Offers resource links, news coverage of global volunteering efforts, and lists of activities and partnerships around the globe.

www.crossculturalsolutions.org—Offers global volunteer/work abroad opportunities in China, Peru, Russia, Ghana, Costa Rica, and India. Also provides resource links to other volunteer programs and general volunteering advice.

Publications

Alternatives to the Peace Corps: A Directory of Third World and U.S. Volunteer Opportunities, edited by Joan Powell. Institute for Food & Development Policy, 2001. Includes helpful sections on evaluating organizations and bringing the lessons that you have learned back home. Also contains an excellent resource section.

How to Live Your Dream of Volunteering Overseas, by Joseph Collins, Stefano DeZerega, and Zahara Heckscher. Penguin USA, 2002. Comprehensive guide to international volunteerism.

So You Want to Join the Peace Corps: What to Know Before You Go, by Dillon Banerjee. Ten Speed Press, 2000. An insider's perspective on what really happens in the Peace Corps, as written by a former Corps participant.

A Peace Corps Chronicle, by Moritz Thomsen. University of Washington Press, 1990. A chronicle of what truly goes on in the Peace Corps, as written by a former participant. Offers a comprehensive account of the ins and outs of a living a Peace Corps lifestyle.

Programs

Amigos de las Americas. Interns aged sixteen and up work for four to eight weeks as summer volunteers on public-health projects in Latin America. (800) 231-7796. www.amigoslink.org.

Interns for Peace. A community-sponsored program dedicated to building trust among Jews and Arabs in Israel through a variety of projects. (212) 870-2226. www.internsforpeace.org.

Partnership for Service Learning. Offers combined study and intercultural experience through community service. Destinations include the Czech Republic, Ecuador, Britain, France, India, Israel, Mexico, and the Philippines. (212) 986-0989. www.ipsl.org.

Peace Corps. Volunteers serve for twenty-seven months and receive intensive language training and cultural orientation. Room and board is provided, and a stipend is awarded at the end of service. The Peace Corps has projects throughout the world. (800) 424-8580. www.peacecorps.gov.

UNIPAL (Universities Educational Fund for Palestinian Refugees). Sends volunteers to teach English to Palestinians and help with handicapped children in the Occupied Territories and Jordan. BCM Unipal, London, WCN 3XX, United Kingdom. www.unipal.org.uk.

Volunteers for Peace. VFP organizes work camps in the U.S. and abroad. Each summer, small groups of young people from around the world come together in European countries and elsewhere to work on community service projects. VFP work camps involve construction, restoration, agricultural, and maintenance projects. After you pay a registration fee and pay for your transportation, the program covers your room, board, and weekend trips. (802) 259-2759. www.vfp.org.

World Teach. Helps students obtain volunteer teaching jobs in developing countries. Undergrads who lack a bachelor's degree are eligible for summer-intern placements. World Teach also publishes a useful pamphlet, *Fundraising Suggestions for World Teach Volunteers.* (617) 495-5527. www.worldteach.org.

Study

Study in the United States

Programs

The Archaeological Institute of America. The AIA publishes an annual *Archaeological Fieldwork Opportunities Bulletin,* a must for anyone considering work on a site. Call (800) 791-9354 to order the book.

Earthwatch. Sponsors scientific expeditions in sixty countries and twenty states. Volunteers are required to pay their own costs, which include food, lodging, and travel to the site. The fee you pay to Earthwatch is considered a tax-deductible donation, so you may be able to funnel payment through your parents and save some money that way. Earthwatch is a membership organization, and it puts out a magazine every two months detailing some of its field opportunities. (800) 776-0188. www.earthwatch.org.

University of California Research Expeditions Program. Its aim is to preserve endangered natural resources by building partnerships between participants, researchers, and the host country populace. Many other schools with large biology, ecology, and archaeology departments have similar clearinghouses for information on these kinds of expeditions. Call your local college or university for more information. (530) 757-3529.

Study Abroad

Programs

American International Youth Student Exchange Program. AIYSEP sends students to Europe, Australia, New Zealand, and the former Soviet Union for a semester or a year on a home-stay exchange program. Students attend classes at local public high schools. Financial aid is available. (415) 499-7669. www.aiysep.org.

AFS (formerly American Field Studies) Intercultural Programs. AFS arranges exchanges for high school students in dozens of countries. Students live with a family and take classes at the local high school. Financial aid is available. (212) 299-9000. www.afs.org.

The Rotary Club. Rotary is an international service organization whose members are usually businesspeople. Local branches sponsor exchanges for students who have not yet attended college. Rotary provides students with airfare, room, board, and a small stipend. (847) 866-3000. www.rotary.org.

Nacel Open Door. Sponsors study programs in Europe and Australia. Financial aid is available. (800) NACELLE. www.nacelopendoor.org.

Semester at Sea. Students spend six weeks on land studying oceanography and nautical science and then spend six weeks sailing on one of the program's two boats. Financial aid is available. Contact the Sea Education Association for more information. (412) 648-7490. www.semesteratsea.com.

CIEE (Council on International Educational Exchange). An incredibly helpful organization that has many publications for people who want to work, travel, or study abroad. Call for a current catalog of publications. (800) 40-STUDY. www.ciee.org.

Travel/Outdoor Adventure

Travel/Outdoor Adventure in the United States

Programs

National Outdoor Leadership School. NOLS offers wilderness education expeditions in the U.S. and abroad. The trips emphasize the acquisition of basic outdoor skills and teach students how to make a minimum impact on the environment. Programs range in length from two weeks to a semester. Financial aid is available. (307) 332-5300. www.nols.edu.

Outward Bound. Outward Bound runs challenging outdoor education programs that range in length from three weeks to a semester. (888) 882-6863. www.outwardbound.org.

Appalachian Mountain Club. This is the organization that promotes and maintains the Appalachian Trail. It can suggest the best books to read before heading out on a hike. (304) 535-6331. www.appalachiantrail.org.

Club Med. Club Med has job opportunities of varying lengths at their luxury resorts around the world. They hire year-round for positions ranging from snorkeling instructors to tour guides. This probably won't be the greatest cultural experience of your life, but it should be a lot of fun. You must be at least nineteen years old and willing to go anywhere in the world to work. Fax: (305) 476-4100. www.clubmedjobs.com.

Publication

Rolling Nowhere, by Ted Conover. Penguin, 1982. The book Ted wrote about his experiences riding freight trains with hoboes.

Travel/Outdoor Adventure Abroad

Publication

The Back Door Guide to Short-Term Job Adventures: Internships, Extraordinary Experiences, Seasonal Jobs, Volunteering, Work Abroad, by Michael Landes. Ten Speed Press, 2001. More than 1,000 listings of short-term work-and-learn adventures. Hundreds of quotes, tips, features, stories, and listings. An invaluable guide for the true adventurer.

Programs

Council Travel. This travel agency, with offices in most large cities and college towns, specializes in students traveling on the cheap. They know more about getting to faraway places cheaply than just about anyone. (800) 2-COUNCIL. www.counciltravel.com.

International Youth Hostel Federation. IYHF runs a worldwide network of hostels where you can stay inexpensively and meet other travelers. +44 1707 324170. www.iyhf.org

Consultants

Robert Gilpin, *Where Are You Headed?* provides consultation to students and their families about alternatives to mainstream education. The service is designed to serve students and their families who are looking for information and advice about the passage through high school and college—and all the twists and turns in between. Six-month membership: $80. Full-year membership: $120. Subscriptions provide access to all features of Whereyouheaded.com. Benefits include complete access to database materials; access to a variety of members-only site features, ranging from useful Web links to college application advice; free e-mail consultations with the Where Are You Headed? staff; and members-only telephone consultations, at additional cost, to be arranged through the website. (617) 698-8977. www.whereyouheaded.com.

Cornelius Bull, Center for Interim Programs works with high school graduates pursuing a year off before college, college students taking a break from higher learning, recent graduates or career-changers casting about for direction, teachers on sabbatical, and so on. The center believes that everyone, at some point in their lives, could gain wisdom, perspective, and experience by taking the time to pursue structured Interim opportunities. Interim's files encompass almost 3,500 programs and more than 3,000 Interim students. There are two offices—one in Cambridge, Massachusetts, and another in Princeton, New Jersey. INTERIM's consulting fee is $1,900 (nonrefundable). (617) 547-0980. www.interimprograms.com.

LEAP*Now* exists to give people of all ages the vision, encouragement, and resources they need to live a creative, fulfilled, and engaged life. Time off for travel, adventure, cultural immersion, real work, intensive experiential study, or learning a language serves to renew your perspective, clarify what is important, and help you find the "juice" in your life. LEAPNow is a broker for such experiences and gives you intelligent access to thousands of possibilities throughout the world. This is as helpful for those overwhelmed by today's information glut as it is for those who don't have enough access to interesting options or who simply don't know how much is available to them. Payment of fee ($1,900) entitles you to LEAPNow information, consultation, and placements for a two-year period starting from the date of the consultation. The fee starts the LEAPNow placement process and is nonrefundable unless they are unable to make a placement for you (this has occurred once in the past five years). LEAPNow offers a reduced fee of $950 for those who are looking for placements of four months' duration or less. (707) 829-1142. www.leapnow.org.

About the Authors

Colin Hall and Ron Lieber grew up together in Chicago, where they attended the Francis W. Parker School for fourteen years. Colin took time off to work and then travel before joining Ron at Amherst. Ron now works as a reporter for *The Wall Street Journal*. He is also the author of *Upstart Start-Ups*, a book about young entrepreneurs. Colin worked on Wall Street after Amherst and is currently a student at Stanford Graduate School of Business.

Notes

Notes

Notes

Notes

Notes

Notes

Notes

Notes

Graduate School Entrance Tests

Business School

Is an MBA in your future? If so, you'll need to take the GMAT. The GMAT is a computer-based test offered year round, on most days of the week. October and November are the most popular months for testing appointments. Most business schools require you to have a few years of work experience before you apply, but that doesn't mean you should put off taking the GMAT. Scores are valid for up to five years, so you should take the test while you're still in college and in the test-taking frame of mind.

Law School

If you want to be able to call yourself an "esquire", you'll need to take the LSAT. Most students take the LSAT in the fall of their senior year—either the October or the December administration. The test is also offered in February and in June. The June test is the only afternoon administration – so if your brain doesn't start functioning until the P.M., this might be the one for you. Just make sure to take it in June of your junior year if you want to meet the application deadlines.

Medical School

The MCAT is offered twice each year, in April and in August. It's a beastly eight-hour exam, but it's a necessary evil if you want to become a doctor. Since you'll need to be familiar with the physics, chemistry, and biology tested on the exam, you'll probably want to wait until April of your junior year to take the test— that's when most students take the MCAT. If you wait until August to give it a shot, you'll still be able to meet application deadlines, but you won't have time to take it again if you're not satisfied with your results.

Other Graduate and Ph.D. Programs

For any other graduate or Ph.D. program, be it art history or biochemical engineering, you'll need to take the GRE General Test. This is another computer-based test, and, like the GMAT, it's offered year-round on most days of the week. The most popular test dates are in late summer and in the fall. Take the test no later than October or November before you plan to enter graduate school to ensure that you meet all application deadlines (and the all-important financial aid deadlines) and to leave yourself some room to take it again if you're not satisfied with your scores.

Understanding the Tests

MCAT

Structure and Format

The Medical College Admission Test (MCAT) is a six-hour paper-and-pencil exam that can take up to eight or nine hours to administer.

The MCAT consists of four scored sections that always appear in the same order:

1. Physical Sciences: 100 minutes; 77 physics and general chemistry questions

2. Verbal Reasoning: 85 minutes; 60 questions based on nine passages

3. Writing Sample: two 30-minute essays

4. Biological Sciences: 100 minutes; 77 biology and organic chemistry questions

Scoring

The Physical Sciences, Biological Sciences, and Verbal Reasoning sections are each scored on a scale of 1 to 15, with 8 as the average score. These scores will be added together to form your Total Score. The Writing Sample is scored from J (lowest) to T (highest), with O as the average score.

Test Dates

The MCAT is offered twice each year—in April and August.

Registration

The MCAT is administered and scored by the MCAT Program Office under the direction of the AAMC. To request a registration packet, you can write to the MCAT Program Office, P.O. Box 4056, Iowa City, Iowa 52243 or call 319-337-1357.

GRE

Structure and Format

The Graduate Record Examinations (GRE) General Test is a multiple-choice test for applicants to graduate school that is taken on computer. It is a computer-adaptive test (CAT), consisting of three sections.

- One 30-minute, 30-question "Verbal Ability" (vocabulary and reading) section

- One 45-minute, 28-question "Quantitative Ability" (math) section

- An Analytical Writing Assessment, consisting of two essay tasks

  o One 45-minute "Analysis of an Issue" task

  o One 30-minute "Analysis of an Argument" task

The GRE is a computer-adaptive test, which means that it uses your performance on previous questions to determine which question you will be asked next. The software calculates your score based on the number of questions you answer correctly, the difficulty of the questions you answer, and the number of questions you complete. Questions that appear early in the test impact your score to a greater degree than do those that come toward the end of the exam.

Scoring

You will receive a Verbal score and a Math score, each ranging from 200 to 800, as well as an Analytic Writing Assessment (AWA) score ranging from 0 to 6.

Test Dates

The GRE is offered year-round in testing centers, by appointment.

Registration

To register for the GRE, call 1-800-GRE-CALL or register online at www.GRE.org.

Understanding the Tests

LSAT

Structure and Format

The Law School Admission Test (LSAT) is a four-hour exam comprised of five 35-minute multiple-choice test sections of approximately 25 questions each, plus an essay:

- Reading Comprehension (1 section)
- Analytical Reasoning (1 section)
- Logical Reasoning (2 sections)
- Experimental Section (1 section)

Scoring

- Four of the five multiple-choice sections count toward your final LSAT score
- The fifth multiple-choice section is an experimental section used solely to test new questions for future exams
- Correct responses count equally and no points are deducted for incorrect or blank responses
- Test takers get a final, scaled score between 120 and 180
- The essay is not scored, and is rarely used to evaluate your candidacy by admissions officers

Test Dates

The LSAT is offered four times each year—in February, June, October, and December.

Registration

To register for the LSAT, visit www.LSAC.org to order a registration book or to register online.

GMAT

Structure and Format

The Graduate Management Admission Test (GMAT) is a multiple-choice test for applicants to business school that is taken on computer. It is a computer-adaptive test (CAT), consisting of three sections:

- Two 30-minute essays to be written on the computer: Analysis of an Argument and Analysis of an Issue
- One 75-minute, 37-question Math section: Problem Solving and Data Sufficiency
- One 75-minute, 41-question Verbal section: Sentence Corrections, Critical Reasoning, and Reading Comprehension

The GMAT is a computer-adaptive test, which means that it uses your performance on previous questions to determine which question you will be asked next. The software calculates your score based on the number of questions you answer correctly, the difficulty of the questions you answer, and the number of questions you complete. Questions that appear early in the test impact your score to a greater degree than do those that come toward the end of the exam.

Scoring

You will receive a composite score ranging from 200 to 800 in 10-point increments, in addition to a Verbal score and a Math score, each ranging from 0 to 60. You will also receive an Analytic Writing Assessment (AWA) score ranging from 0 to 6.

Test Dates

The GMAT is offered year-round in testing centers, by appointment.

Registration

To register for the GMAT, call 1-800-GMAT-NOW or register online at www.MBA.com.

Dispelling the Myths about Test Preparation and Admissions

MYTH: If you have a solid GPA, your test score isn't as important for getting into a college or graduate school.

FACT: While it is true that admissions committees consider several factors in their admissions decisions, including test scores, GPA, work or extra-curricular experience, and letters of recommendation, it is not always true that committees will overlook your test scores if you are strong in other areas. Particularly for large programs with many applicants, standardized tests are often the first factor that admissions committees use to evaluate prospective students.

MYTH: Standardized exams test your basic skills or innate ability; therefore your score cannot be significantly improved through studying.

FACT: Nothing could be farther from the truth. You can benefit tremendously from exposure to actual tests and expert insight into the test writers' habits and the most commonly used tricks.

MYTH: There are lots of skills you can learn to help you improve your math score, but you can't really improve your verbal score.

FACT: The single best way to improve your verbal score is to improve your vocabulary. Question types in the verbal reasoning sections of standardized tests all rely upon your understanding of the words in the questions and answer choices. If you know what the words mean, you'll be able to answer the questions quickly and accurately. Improving your critical reading skills is also very important.

MYTH: Standardized exams measure your intelligence.

FACT: While test scores definitely matter, they do NOT test your intelligence. The scores you achieve reflect only how prepared you were to take that particular exam and how good a test taker you are.

Hyperlearning *MCAT Prep Course*

The Princeton Review Difference

Nearly 40% of all MCAT test takers take the exam twice due to inadequate preparation the first time. **Do not be one of them.**

Our Approach to Mastering the MCAT

You will need to conquer both the verbal and the science portions of the MCAT to get your best score. But it might surprise you to learn that the Verbal Reasoning and Writing Sample are the most important sub-sections on the test. That is why we dedicate twice as much class time to these sections as does any other national course! We will help you to develop superlative reading and writing skills so you will be ready to write well crafted, concise essay responses. And of course, we will also help you to develop a thorough understanding of the basic science concepts and problem-solving techniques that you will need to ace the MCAT.

Total Preparation: 41 Class Sessions

With 41 class sessions, our MCAT course ensures that you will be prepared and confident by the time you take the test.

The Most Practice Materials

You will receive more than 3,000 pages of practice materials and 1,300 pages of supplemental materials, and all are yours to keep. Rest assured that our material is always fresh. Each year we write a new set of practice passages to reflect the style and content of the most recent tests. You will also take five full-length practice MCATs under actual testing conditions, so you can build your test-taking stamina and get used to the time constraints.

Specialist Instructors

Your course will be led by a team of between two and five instructors—each an expert in his or her specific subjects. Our instructors are carefully screened and undergo a rigorous national training program. In fact, the quality of our instructors is a major reason students recommend our course to their friends.

Get the Score You Want

We guarantee you will be completely satisfied with your MCAT score!* Our students boast an average MCAT score improvement of ten points.**

*If you attend all class sessions, complete all tests and homework, finish the entire course, take the MCAT at the next administration and do not void your test, and you still are not satisfied with your score, we will work with you again at no additional cost for one of the next two MCAT administrations.
**Independently verified by International Communications Research.

ClassSize-8 *Classroom Courses for the GRE, LSAT, and GMAT*

Small Classes

We know students learn better in smaller classes. With no more than eight students in a Princeton Review class, your instructor knows who you are, and works closely with you to identify your strengths and weaknesses. You will be as prepared as possible. When it comes to your future, you shouldn't be lost in a crowd of students.

Guaranteed Satisfaction

A prep course is a big investment—in terms of both time and money. At The Princeton Review, your investment will pay off. Our LSAT students improve by an average of 7 points, our GRE students improve by an average of 212 points, and our GMAT students boast an average score improvement of 92.5 points—the best score improvement in the industry.* We guarantee that you will be satisfied with your results. If you're not, we'll work with you again for free.**

Expert Instructors

Princeton Review instructors are energetic and smart—they've all scored in the 95th percentile or higher on standardized tests. Our instructors will make your experience engaging and effective.

Free Extra Help

We want you to get your best possible score on the test. If you need extra help on a particular topic, your instructor is happy to meet with you outside of class to make sure you are comfortable with the material—at no extra charge!

Online Lessons, Tests, and Drills

Princeton Review *ClassSize-8* Courses are the only classroom courses that have online lessons designed to support each class session. You can practice concepts you learn in class, spend some extra time on topics that you find challenging, or prepare for an upcoming class. And you'll have access as soon as you enroll, so you can get a head start on your test preparation.

The Most Comprehensive, Up-to-Date Materials

Our research and development team studies the tests year-round to stay on top of trends and to make sure you learn what you need to get your best score.

*Independently verified by International Communications Research (ICR).

**Some restrictions apply.

Online *and* LiveOnline *Courses*

for the GRE, LSAT, and GMAT

The Best of Both Worlds

We've combined our high-quality, comprehensive test preparation with a convenient, multimedia format that works around your schedule and your needs.

Online *and* LiveOnline *Courses*

Lively, Engaging Lessons

If you think taking an online course means staring at a screen and struggling to pay attention, think again. Our lessons are engaging and interactive – you'll never just read blocks of text or passively watch video clips. Princeton Review online courses feature animation, audio, interactive lessons, and self-directed navigation.

Customized, Focused Practice

The course software will discover your personal strengths and weaknesses. It will help you to prioritize and focus on the areas that are most important to your success. Of course, you'll have access to dozens of hours' worth of lessons and drills covering all areas of the test, so you can practice as much or as little as you choose.

Help at your Fingertips

Even though you'll be working on your own, you won't be left to fend for yourself. We're ready to help at any time of the day or night: you can chat online with a live Coach, check our Frequently Asked Questions database, or talk to other students in our discussion groups.

LiveOnline *Course*

Extra Features

In addition to self-directed online lessons, practice tests, drills, and more, you'll participate in five live class sessions and three extra help sessions given in real time over the Internet. You'll get the live interaction of a classroom course from the comfort of your own home.

ExpressOnline *Course*

The Best in Quick Prep

If your test is less than a month away, or you just want an introduction to our legendary strategies, this mini-course may be the right choice for you. Our multimedia lessons will walk you through basic test-taking strategies to give you the edge you need on test day.

1-2-1 *Private Tutoring*

The Ultimate in Personalized Attention

If you're too busy for a classroom course, prefer learning at your kitchen table, or simply want your instructor's undivided attention, *1-2-1* Private Tutoring may be for you.

Focused on You

In larger classrooms, there is always one student who monopolizes the instructor's attention. With *1-2-1* Private Tutoring, that student is you. Your instructor will tailor the course to your needs – greater focus on the subjects that cause you trouble, and less focus on the subjects that you're comfortable with. You can get all the instruction you need in less time than you would spend in a class.

Expert Tutors

Our outstanding tutoring staff is comprised of specially selected, rigorously trained instructors who have performed exceptionally in the classroom. They have scored in the top percentiles on standardized tests and received the highest student evaluations.

Schedules to Meet Your Needs

We know you are busy, and preparing for the test is perhaps the last thing you want to do in your "spare" time. The Princeton Review *1-2-1* Private Tutoring Program will work around your schedule.

Additional Online Lessons and Resources

The learning continues outside of your tutoring sessions. Within the Online Student Center*, you will have access to math, verbal, AWA, and general strategy lessons to supplement your private instruction. Best of all, they are accessible to you 24 hours a day, 7 days a week.

*Available for LSAT, GRE, and GMAT

The Princeton Review Admissions Services

At The Princeton Review, we care about your ability to get accepted to the best school for you. But, we all know getting accepting involves much more than just doing well on standardized tests. That's why, in addition to our test preparation services, we also offer free admissions services to students looking to enter college or graduate school. You can find these services on our website, *www.PrincetonReview.com*, the best online resource for researching, applying to, and learning how to pay for the right school for you.

No matter what type of program you're applying to—undergraduate, graduate, law, business, or medical—**PrincetonReview.com has the free tools, services, and advice you need to navigate the admissions process.** Read on to learn more about the services we offer.

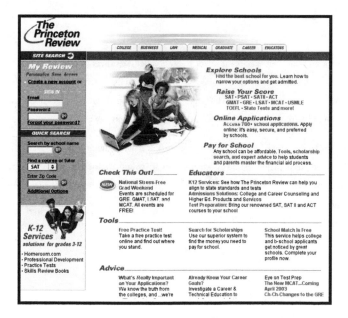

Research Schools
www.PrincetonReview.com/Research

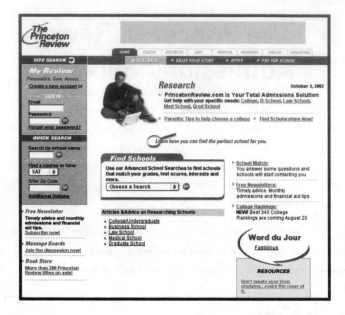

PrincetonReview.com features an interactive tool called **Advanced School Search.** When you use this tool, you enter stats and information about yourself to find a list of schools that fit your needs. From there you can read statistical and editorial information about thousands of colleges and universities. In addition, you can find out what currently enrolled college students say about their schools.

Our **College Majors Search** is one of the most popular features we offer. Here you can read profiles on hundreds of majors to find information on curriculum, salaries, careers, and the appropriate high school preparation, as well as colleges that offer it. From the Majors Search, you can investigate corresponding Careers, read **Career Profiles**, and learn what career is the best match for you by taking our **Career Quiz**.

Another powerful tool we feature is **School Match**. You tell us your scores, interests, and preferences and Princeton Review partner schools will contact you.

No matter what type of school or specialized program you are considering, **PrincetonReview.com has free articles and advice, in addition to our tools, to help you make the right choice.**

Apply to School
www.PrincetonReview.com/Apply

For most students, completing the school application is the most stressful part of the admissions process. PrincetonReview.com's powerful **Online School Application Engine** makes it easy to apply.

Paper applications are mostly a thing of the past. And, our hundreds of partner schools tell us they prefer to receive your applications online.

Using our online application service is simple:

- Enter information once and the common data automatically transfers onto each application.
- Save your applications and access them at any time to edit and perfect.
- Submit electronically or print and mail in.
- Pay your application fee online, using an e-check, or mail the school a check.

Our powerful application engine is built to accommodate all your needs.

Pay for School
www.PrincetonReview.com/Finance

The financial aid process is confusing for everyone. But don't worry. Our free online tools, services, and advice can help you plan for the future and get the money you need to pay for school.

Our **Scholarship Search** engine will help you find free money, although often scholarships alone won't cover the cost of high tuitions. So, we offer other tools and resources to help you navigate the entire process.

Filling out the FAFSA can be a daunting process, use our **FAFSA Worksheet** to make sure you answer the questions correctly the first time.

If scholarships and government aid aren't enough to swing the cost of tuition, we'll help you secure student loans. The Princeton Review has partnered with a select group of reputable financial institutions who will help **explore all your loans options**.

If you know how to work the financial aid process, you'll learn you don't have to **eliminate a school based on tuition.**

Be a Part of the PrincetonReview.com Community

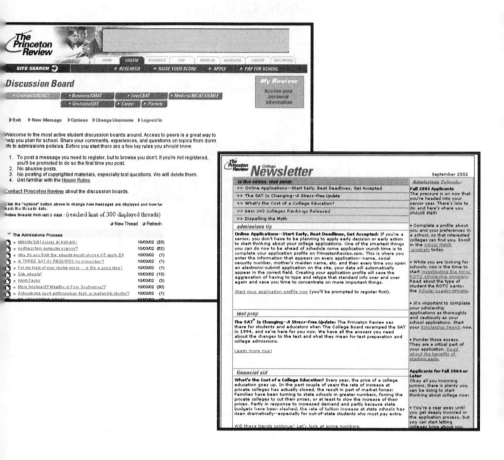

PrincetonReview.com's **Discussion Boards** and **Free Newsletters** are additional services to help you to get information about the admissions process from your peers and from The Princeton Review experts.

Book Store
www.PrincetonReview.com/college/Bookstore.asp

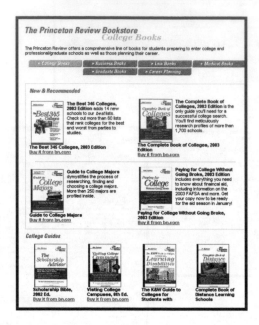

In addition to this book, we publish hundreds of other titles, including guidebooks that highlight life on campus, student opinion, and all the statistical data that you need to know about any school you are considering. Just a few of the titles that we offer are:

- Complete Book of Business Schools
- Complete Book of Law Schools
- Complete Book of Medical Schools
- The Best 345 Colleges
- The K&W Guide to Colleges for Students with Learning Disabilities or Attention Deficit Disorder
- Guide to College Majors
- Paying for College Without Going Broke

For a complete listing of all of our titles, visit our **online book store**:

http://www.princetonreview.com/college/bookstore.asp